Signs of
Hope

Also by Alejandro Bullón:

The Invitation

Knowing Jesus Is Everything

To order, call **1–800–765–6955.** Visit us at
www.reviewandherald.com for information on other
Review and Herald® products.

Signs of Hope

ALEJANDRO BULLÓN

REVIEW AND HERALD® PUBLISHING ASSOCIATION
Since 1861 | www.reviewandherald.com

Copyright © 2008 by Review and Herald® Publishing Association

Published by Review and Herald® Publishing Association, Hagerstown, MD 21741-1119

All rights reserved. No portion of this book may be reproduced, stored in a retrieval system, or transmitted in any form or by any means (electronic, mechanical, photocopy, recording, scanning, or other), except for brief quotations in critical reviews or articles, without the prior written permission of the publisher.

Review and Herald® titles may be purchased in bulk for educational, business, fund-raising, or sales promotional use. For information, e-mail SpecialMarkets@reviewandherald.com.

The Review and Herald® Publishing Association publishes biblically based materials for spiritual, physical, and mental growth and Christian discipleship.

The author assumes full responsibility for the accuracy of all facts and quotations as cited in this book.

Unless otherwise indicated, Scripture quotations are from the *New American Standard Bible,* copyright © 1960, 1962, 1963, 1968, 1971, 1972, 1973, 1975, 1977, 1994 by the Lockman Foundation. Used by permission.

Texts credited to Message are from *The Message.* Copyright © 1993, 1994, 1995, 1996, 2000, 2001, 2002 . Used by permission of NavPress Publishing Group.

This book was
Edited by Gerald Wheeler
Copyedited by James Cavil
Translated by Loron Wade
Designed by Ron J. Pride
Cover photo credits:
    Sunset: © iStockphoto.com/anp
    Mountaintop: © iStockphoto.com/kemie
    Cliff texture: © iStockphoto.com/Adventure Photo
Interior designed by Heather Rogers
Typeset:Bembo 11/13

PRINTED IN U.S.A.

12   11   10   09   08   10 9 8 7 6 5 4 3 2 1

Library of Congress Cataloging-in-Publication Data
Bullon, Alejandro, 1947-   .
  Signs of hope / Allejandro Bullon.
      p. cm.
  1. Eschatology. 2. Adventists—Doctrines. 3. Seventh-Day Adventists—Doctrines.
I. Title.
   BT821.3.B85 2008
   236—dc22

                                        2008039427

ISBN 978-0-8280-2392-4

Contents

Introduction 7

1. What Is the Sign of Your Coming?..............11

2. Wars and Rumors of Wars 17

3. False Christs and False Prophets 26

4. Religious Skepticism and Secularism............39

5. Earthquakes and Hurricanes 57

6. A Heartless Society 66

7. A Sex-obsessed Generation 75

8. Economic Recession 85

9. The Preaching of the Gospel........................94

10. A Strange Persecution 103

11. When Will Jesus Return? 117

Introduction

Then He told them a parable: "Behold the fig tree
and all the trees; as soon as they put forth leaves,
you see it and know for yourselves that summer is now near.
So you also, when you see these things happening,
recognize that the kingdom of God is near"
(Luke 21:29-31).

Trim and physically fit at 70 years old, his hair and beard whitened by time, the man with a gentle face moved at a steady pace. He looked like a loving grandfather on his way to bring a present to his grandchildren. At least, that's what anyone would think seeing him walk down the streets of the city in his dark suit, a leather briefcase in his right hand.

But the truth is different. The man didn't have a present for anyone. His briefcase hid a bomb—that is, a "bomb" in the form of the news he was carrying. It was news that would shake public opinion around the world and stir up controversy. As the news spread, a lot of people thought the old fellow was crazy. Others believed that he was engaged in an exercise of self-promotion. At any rate, Ernie Chambers, independent state senator in Nebraska, was known as an old, argumentative, and irreverent politician.

On that morning of September 14, 2007, Senator Chambers went into the Douglas County courthouse and filed a lawsuit against God. He demanded that God stop causing so much terror in the world.

In the petition that he filed the African-American

attorney who had never practiced law accused God of causing "fearsome floods, egregious earthquakes, horrendous hurricanes, terrifying tornadoes, pestilential plagues, ferocious famines, devastating droughts, genocidal wars, birth defects and the like." He said the Deity was responsible for "calamitous catastrophes resulting in the widespread death, destruction, and terrorization of millions upon millions of the earth's inhabitants, including innocent babes, infants, children, the aged and infirm, without mercy or distinction,"[1] and he asked the court for an injunction ordering God to cease and desist.

Strange or quixotic though it may appear, Chambers' lawsuit against God shows at least two things: the irreverence of modern humanity, and, more significantly, the anxiety that millions of people feel today because of the terrifying events taking place all around them. Strange things are, indeed, happening to our planet.

At no previous time in recorded history have we seen so many natural disasters in such a short period of time. They have leveled entire cities and snuffed out thousands of lives. According to a report of the United Nations International Panel on Climate Change, if global warming continues at its present rate, it could eradicate a fourth of the species of plants and animals of the earth by the year 2050. [2]

We can no longer fail to be concerned about such news. Senator Chambers' lawsuit may appear frivolous or absurd, but it is coherent in its concern.

The atmospheric phenomena threatening the safety of the planet are nothing less than terrifying. Is something beyond human control about to take place?

If not, how can we explain so many natural disasters, so much suffering and despair? How can we make sense of the scores of floods, earthquakes, fires, volcanoes, and hurricanes? How can we cope with the terror, desolation, and death that face us on every hand? And the existential confusion that people are experiencing? How do we explain so many people destroying lives and dreams without mercy? For example, how could human beings, supposedly the most intelligent of creatures, kidnap innocent children to humiliate them sexually and sell photos of them to the perverse world of pornography? What went on in the mind of a university student who opened fire indiscriminately, killing many of his classmates and afterward taking his own life? What would lead youth today to spend billions of dollars every year on drugs, supporting a vast criminal underworld? What is it that they are looking for so desperately and not finding? Why do they do such things, knowing that they are only destroying themselves? Something is wrong. The train of life has derailed and is hurtling out of control over a precipice.

This book takes a look at what is behind such events. All of the seemingly incoherent acts of humanity and nature do have a rational explanation. Nature out of control, human perversity, senseless wars, and famines and epidemics are only the visible part of what is happening in the world. Behind the curtain of these apparently unrelated facts, something is approaching. As yet invisible and silent, but inexorable. What the present world doesn't understand, a Book predicted centuries ago.

Jesus said: "Learn the parable from the fig tree: when its branch has already become tender and put forth its leaves, you know that summer is near; so, you too, when you see all these things, recognize that He is near, right at the door" (Matthew 24:32, 33).

What is it that is near? What was Jesus talking about when He spoke those words? The answer to these questions will change the course of history. And it will most definitely affect your personal struggles and the destiny of the people you love. This is the story of the climactic end of the millennial conflict. Read this book, and you will understand.

---

[1] www.ketv.com/news/14133442/detail.html. Douglas County District Court Judge Marlon Polk later threw the injuction out because the court did not have an address for God to send it.

[2] *Climate Change, 1995: The Science of Climate Change: Contribution of Working Group I to the Second Assessment Report of the Intergovernmental Panel on Climate Change* (Cambridge: Cambridge University Press, 1996).

One

What Is the Sign of Your Coming?

> *"As He was sitting on the Mount of Olives,*
> *the disciples came to Him privately, saying,*
> *'Tell us, when will these things happen, and what will be*
> *the sign of Your coming, and of the end of the age?'"*
> *(Matthew 24:3).*

The supreme moment was approaching, the critical hour when the King of kings and Lord of lords, the Creator of the universe and owner of the heavens and the earth, would descend to the depths of humiliation. Nailed to a cross reserved for the worst criminal, He would pay the infinite price to ransom the human race. The price would be His own blood. But through that blood He would rescue humanity from the power of death.

A dense cloud of sorrow and suffering hung over the disciples like a messenger of doom. But they did not perceive it. Maybe they were too human to understand the things of the Spirit. The Master, however, was well aware of the solemnity of the hour. While in a short time anguish and loneliness would overwhelm them, He didn't want them to suffer. He loved them with an incomprehensible and infinite love. How could He make them understand so that they would be prepared for what was about to happen?

The Bible account says: "Jesus came out from the temple and was going away when His disciples came up to point out the temple buildings to Him" (Matthew

24:1). "Teacher," they said, "behold what wonderful stones and what wonderful buildings!" (Mark 13:1). Even though the eternal destiny of humanity would be decided in a few hours, the disciples were concerned only about material things—the buildings of the Temple.

The human mind is fascinated by glitter—by the things it can perceive through its senses. The disciples could see the Temple. They could touch the polished blocks of limestone and admire its gold furnishings and mighty columns.

Twenty centuries have passed, and people are still fascinated by what they can perceive with their physical senses. The spiritual dimension of life, however, continues to be elusive. Once again, we are approaching a critical point in history. But the great climax of events that looms just ahead seems to be lost in the shadow of our humanity. The end of time is hovering over us, but like the disciples of old, we're oblivious to it. All our attention is concentrated on the things we can view with our physical eyes—the wars, violence, earthquakes, hurricanes, global warming, social calamities, and injustice that surround us on every side. Those things fill our whole field of vision. But we are blind to their meaning. So we look for quick-fix human solutions to remove the dark shadows that cover the land.

On that occasion, Jesus' answer to His disciples left them perplexed. "Do you not see all these things?" He asked. "Truly I say to you, not one stone here will be left upon another, which will not be torn down" (Matthew 24:2). The disciples heard their Master's words and concluded that when He said that this fabulous building would someday lie in ruins He must have been referring to the cataclysm that would take place at the "end of the age." In their minds, how else could it be any other way? Jesus had talked to them about His return, so they reasoned that it must be at that time—at the end of the age—that the Temple would be destroyed.

Nevertheless, such a thought was extremely painful to the disciples. It hurt them in a way that they didn't know how to explain. All their hopes in life centered on casting off the hated Roman yoke from their nation. For generations their people had been waiting for the Messiah, who would take possession of the Temple and lead the nation to victory. Now Jesus was telling them that the Temple would lie in ruins.

The disciples had left everything they had to follow Jesus. They had accepted Him as Lord of their lives. Now Jesus seemed obsessed with death and destruction. Much as they might try, they couldn't make sense of what He was saying.

That sad afternoon they descended into the Kidron Valley as if they were going down into the valley of death. It was a silent and solemn procession. What Jesus had told them continued to disturb the disciples, but they didn't have the courage to ask Him anything more as they walked along.

As they climbed the slopes of the Mount of Olives they were still troubled. When they had seated themselves on the mountainside, they returned to the theme of the destruction of the Temple, opening their hearts to Jesus. "Tell us, when will these things happen, and what will be the sign of Your coming, and of the end of the age?" (Matthew 24:3).

13

Then the Lord began to paint a picture of the world situation that would precede His return to earth. He talked to them about wars, rumors of wars, earthquakes, false christs, and of persecution to come.

Jesus had a special message for the disciples. They would be witnesses to the Roman fury that would destroy the Temple only about 40 years later. Part of the signs of Matthew 24 refer to what would happen just before the destruction of the Temple. But Jesus had a message for us today as well, because He also announced what would take place at the end of the world.

As in Jesus' time, people today urgently need to read between the lines, to see beyond the terrifying events of our time and understand their meaning. The signs of the return of Christ presented in the Bible are a faithful description of what is happening today, a portrait of the present world and its constant struggles with humanity pitted against itself and with the mad fury of nature that can no longer bear human bondage and is rebelling like a wild colt.

The following is a description of some of the things taking place today, events that will happen more frequently as the end approaches. It is an urgent message. But it is also a message of hope—an announcement of a new day and a new world.

Our planet seems trapped in great darkness. The shadows around us are frightening. But they are also encouraging, because they are an evidence that the King is coming. The glorious dawning will soon be here. Experience has taught us that the denser the darkness, the nearer the new day. The darkness that surrounds us should give us great hope.

I know by personal experience how valuable such hope is. I needed it one night when I was lost in the jungle. I had walked all day, and my strength was gone. The Indian guide who was with me thought it would be best to sleep by the edge of the river.

"Tomorrow will be another day," he told me, "and you will be in better shape. It's useless to continue walking in the darkness."

So we stopped. The darkness seemed to permeate even the air that I breathed. It felt as if it were brushing against my skin. All lives have those nights that are heavy and dark with sadness. Mystic poet Saint John of the Cross called them "dark nights of the soul." That night in the jungle was for me one of those—a night that seemed eternal.

I could not sleep. The night sounds and the darkness seemed threatening. It must have been about 4:00 or 5:00 in the morning when I asked the guide if the night was getting darker or if it was just my imagination.

"It's not just your imagination," he told me. "The night really has gotten darker. That means that in a few minutes the sun will be coming out."

And it was so. Ten minutes later we saw the first rays of dawn, and soon the sun crept over the horizon. When I could see its golden rays smiling at me in the distance, I knew I was safe.

The night of this world is getting darker and darker. Grief, pain, and death surround us. Injustice, misery, and hunger lurk everywhere. At times it seems that all is lost. But it isn't. The night of this world will soon end. The sunlight of a new day will burst on the horizon.

And even while we wait for Jesus' return, He is

15

here with us now. "Stay by My side," He says through His Holy Spirit. "Trust Me to go with you through the hours of darkness that are still ahead."

What will you do? Will you accept His invitation? The answer is yours alone.

Two

Wars and Rumors of Wars

"When you hear of wars and rumors of wars, do not be frightened;
those things must take place; but that is not yet the end. For nation
will rise up against nation, and kingdom against kingdom. . . .
These things are merely the beginning of birth pangs"
(Mark 13:7, 8).

The child stared with terror at the man with the black hood. The weapon pointed at his head filled him with horror, and he trembled. He didn't have the courage to look at the bottle of yellow liquid that he held in his left hand. In desperation he began to cry. What can a 6-year-old child do except cry under such brutal circumstances?

"Drink it or I'll kill you!"

The voice of the big man sounded threatening. Ivan had no other choice as he drank his own urine.

How could we find words to describe such a scene? Anything you could say is too much—or maybe not enough. Better to pretend it didn't happen. Maybe that way we will be less embarrassed to admit that we too are human and that our kind has become little more than animals.

It all happened on a Wednesday, the first of September. The large clock of the central building of the elementary school announced that it was 9:40 in the morning. It was a typical summer morning. In the school the students, teachers, and parents were getting ready to start a program called "Festival of Learning."

17

Suddenly shots rang out, followed by cursing, threats, and blows. In a fraction of a second 32 men and women armed to the teeth, their faces covered by black hoods, seized control of the school. A few minutes later they had in their power 1,300 hostages.[1]

The invaders marched their captives to the school gymnasium and began to lay out an enormous quantity of explosives to protect themselves in case of attack. The special security forces of the national army quickly surrounded the school, prepared to rush in at the first careless move by the terrorists. The hostages will never forget their three days of horror. War had spilled into their peaceful school. Jesus said it a long time ago: "You will be hearing of wars and rumors of wars" (Matthew 24:6). It would be one of the signs that would announce His return to earth.

At first the invaders made no demands. They shot 15-20 men, and threatened to execute 50 hostages every time the security forces killed one of their own number and 20 every time a terrorist was wounded. Their leader announced to the press that he would give the children neither food nor water. Some children would tell later that when they asked for water, the terrorists forced them to drink their own urine.

On Friday, September 3, it was hot. The children were suffocating in the gym. No one imagined the approaching tragedy. (Less than 120 days after this incident another tragedy of catastrophic dimensions would shake the world: a killer tsunami would wipe entire cities off the map and sweep away 200,000 lives.)

The eyes of the world waited to see the outcome of the attack on the defenseless children. Suddenly a bomb exploded. Cries of anguish filled the gymnasium. Special forces took advantage of the panic and rushed in to seize control of the situation. The air stank of gunpowder, blood, and death, as well as terror and desperation. The hostage situation was over. The final result: nearly 400 dead and more than 700 wounded.

But the incident was just one drop in an increasing torrent. People fight and kill each other almost without a reason. As I write these lines news reports have just come in of a pregnant woman assaulted by three men. According to the men they were in a hurry, and she didn't get out of their way fast enough. The time they spent beating up the defenseless woman was much more than the second they would have had to wait for her to get out of the way.

We have grown accustomed to living in a climate of constant hostility. One of the most currently active wars has already cost thousands of lives of innocent people, people who had nothing to do with the political interests involved. At first everyone avidly followed the events of the conflict. Now, in spite of the deaths of dozens every day, people have lost interest. It has become so routine that no one pays attention anymore.

Today no one knows who might be carrying a bomb. The enemy is everywhere and faceless. Everyone is afraid.

Once when I was traveling, a passenger seated beside me in the airplane asked, "Haven't there always been wars since human beings first appeared on earth? Didn't Cain kill his brother Abel? How can 'wars and rumors of wars' be a sign of the Second Coming?"

It is true, of course. Since the entrance of sin people have always lived in a climate of war. It is the result of their own inner struggle—of their conflicts and unhappiness, of their estrangement from God. Nevertheless, never in history has there been so much tension and violence as today.

Two terrible conflicts shook the past century. Up until that time the world had never seen such devastation. World War I killed 20 million people, and World War II 73 million. In a radio transmission from Hiroshima in 1945 after the explosion of the first atomic bomb, William Ripley said: "I am standing on the place where the end of the world began." However, those wars were not the sign of the end. Jesus had said: "You will be hearing of wars and rumors of war. See that you are not frightened, for those things must take place, but that is not yet the end" (verses 6, 7).

The climate of war that is part of our lives today is not limited to international incidents. What weakens the fundamental structure of most countries today is their internal conflicts. International wars are becoming the exception. Of the 56 important armed conflicts recorded in the past decade, only three involved one country against another. All the rest were internal struggles, although in 14 of them foreign troops intervened on one side or another.[2]

On the other hand, while wars between wealthy countries dominated the first half of the past century, the majority of the conflicts of today take place among the poorest of the world. Nations that can't even feed themselves now squander their most precious resources fighting citizen against citizen.[3]

Studies by specialists show a definite relationship

between armed conflicts and world hunger. One problem leads to another. Financial recessions throw millions of people into misery, and hunger follows natural disasters and wars.[4]

In our day many countries suffer from internal conflicts led by the so-called revenge guerrillas. Internal conflicts generally take place in rural areas, where the defenseless subsistence farmers bear the disastrous consequences. The people hurt the most are the least responsible for what is happening.

The guerrillas interrupt food production and cause hunger by looting the crops, cattle, and food reserves of the farmers. The constant movements of the armed revolutionaries keep people from working, discourage agriculture, and disrupt the transportation routes through which farm produce can reach market.

The various factions force young people to join the fighting, removing them from the productive sector of society. The resulting increase in hunger remains long after the violence has passed. What can be done in a land in which goods have been destroyed, people have been killed and wounded, the population has fled to escape the danger, and in which the damage to the environment has become irreparable?[5]

Even worse are the land mines scattered across agricultural land that kill and maim people and discourage them from farming for decades after the conflicts have ceased.

After World War II many believed that the world would have peace. During those years arms expenditure dropped by 37 percent, and people talked of international peace and harmony.[6]

But it turned out to be an illusion! Prophecy had foretold that things would go from bad to worse: "While they are saying, 'Peace and safety!' then destruction will come upon them suddenly" (1 Thessalonians 5:3). And it was true. The dream came to an abrupt end in 1988. Since that year the arms sales around the world have been growing out of control. Today, they amount to the scandalous sum of 835 billion euros per year. That is 15 times more than the total spent on humanitarian and other aid. What is even worse, the expenditure was the greatest in the poorest countries of the world.

New orders in the arms trade have grown exponentially in recent years. Ironically, the five principal providers of arms are all permanent members of the U.N. Security Council. Do you think there will soon be peace at this rate?[7]

"But I don't feel anything like that," a young university student told me the other day.

Maybe you don't feel it either, especially if you live in the city in which guerrilla warfare may be less apparent. But you may be used to another type of violence that you are, in fact, aware of. Do you hesitate to go into dark places when night comes, even around your own neighborhood? Are there areas in your own city that you wouldn't want to venture into even by day? Urban violence, the other unending war, is a constant part of the experience of people who live in the big cities of the world.

We usually think that wars today rage only in the Middle East or in the inaccessible mountain regions where organized guerrillas hide. It is true that the worst war of the early twenty-first century has cost more than 226,000 lives. The dead during the invasion of that country were 11,405, including soldiers, guerrillas, and civilians. But another great country of the world has had a silent war hardly noticed by the news media. It kills 48,000 people a year.[8] During a five-year period 240,000 have died on its violent streets. Organized crime has succeeded in paralyzing an entire megalopolis, killing 20 police officers a day. Truck hijacking has a stranglehold on the roads, drugs trafficking controls the poor neighborhoods, and arms trafficking and contraband are rampant. And all of that generates panic among the citizens. Nevertheless, the country is "not at war."[9]

With an average of 500 kidnappings per month (more than 16 a day), another great metropolis is considered one of most dangerous cities in the world. In that city the kidnapping industry costs $70 million a year, and the middle class is obliged to use special armor as a normal accessory on their vehicles.[10]

The situation is similar in many other great cities of the planet. In the past year 4.2 million people became victims of crime in one city alone. Any other metropolis of the world could show equally startling statistics. For many millions of people violence on the streets is a grotesque part of their daily lives.[11]

We see the words of Jesus being fulfilled on a daily basis. Wars and rumors of wars, fratricidal conflicts, and senseless destruction take place on every hand. Thinking men and women everywhere are trying to understand what is happening, but they can't make sense of it.

In 1984 I led in an evangelistic crusade in the

National Stadium of Lima, Peru. Forty thousand people filled the stadium night after night. They were eager to hear the good news of the gospel. One month later I received a letter from a member of the guerilla movement that had brought so much suffering to my people. "I went to the National Stadium, not because I was interested in what you had to say," the writer declared. "I was there fulfilling a mission assigned by my group. We are everywhere present, with our eyes and ears open. I went to the stadium fulfilling a routine duty. I am not an evil person. I simply am a dreamer. I dream of a free country, in which children are born with hope and not condemned to a life of exploitation and suffering. Unfortunately, to build that country it is necessary to destroy the established society. I thought that in order to do that I had to pay the price, and that price is the shedding of innocent blood. But that night I heard you talk about Jesus. I understood that all the blood that was necessary has already been shed on the cross of Calvary. But what do you want me to do now with the memory of my crimes? What can I do with the nightmares that scream at me every time I try to sleep? How can I get out of my mind the image of innocent people pleading on their knees for me not kill them? Where can I go with my pain, with my past, with the terrible weight of my guilt?"

It was a cry of desperation from a human heart. What can I do? Where can I go? In the midst of that whirlwind of struggles and afflictions, I invite you to listen to the gentle voice of Jesus: "Peace I leave with you; My peace I give to you; not as the world gives do

I give to you. Do not let your heart be troubled, nor let it be fearful" (John 14:27). During the time of conflict and war in which we live, there could never be a better invitation.

Will you accept it?

The answer is yours alone.

---

[1] José Eduardo Varela, "O masacre dos Inocentes," *Revista VEJA,* Sept. 12, 2004.

[2] Sigrun Mogedal, deputy minister of Foreign Affairs for Norway, "The Economics of Civil War" (document presented at the World Bank Conference on the Economics and Politics of Civil War, Oslo, Norway, 2001).

[3] *Ibid.*

[4] "Rome Declaration on World Food Security: World Food Summit Declaration and Plan of Action" (United Nations Food and Agriculture Organization, June 10-13, 2002).

[5] More than 4 million people have died in violent conflicts since 1989, and 37 million have had to flee as refugees. Land mines claim more than 25,000 victims per year, hindering reconstruction and development (World Bank, 2000).

[6] I have obtained the information on military spending and arms trading from the following sources: *Conversion Survey, 2001* (Bonn: International Center for Conversion, 2001); *The Military Balance 2001-2002* (International Institute for Strategic Studies); Data Base of World Military Expenditure and Arms (Arms Control and Disarmament Agency of the United States).

[7] Juan Carlos Casté, "World Food Conference" (Rome: 1974); www.catolicismo.com.br/.

[8] "Violencia: O Qué fazer?"; http://opiniaopublica.com.br/interna.php.

[9] *Ibid.*

[10] "Indústria do Secuestro Asola América Latina"; www.forum seguranca.org.br/.

[11] "Situación actual de la delincuencia en México"; www.cam pusanuncios.com/detanuncio-91009X-situacion-actual-Madrid.html.

Three

False Christs and False Prophets

"For false Christs and false prophets will arise and will show great signs and wonders, so as to mislead, if possible, even the elect" (Matthew 24:24).

As he moves with carefully studied gestures his speech mingles irony and bravado. A watch set with diamonds adorns his wrist, he travels from place to place in luxurious vehicles, and he lives in a $7 million mansion. He says he is the Christ reincarnate. When journalists ask why he uses expensive clothing when Jesus walked on the earth with an old tunic and a pair of worn sandals, he replies: "In my first coming I was here to suffer and die. Now I have come back to reign."

Born in Puerto Rico, José Luis Miranda has two tattoos with the numbers 666 on his forearm. He claims to be both Christ and the antichrist because he teaches a different message from the one proclaimed by the suffering Jesus. "Now," according to Miranda, he is "a king reincarnate and victorious."[1]

And he's not the only one. In a house in Boqueirão, Curitiba, in Brazil, a curtain opens and there appears decked out in a white tunic and a red cape, with a crown of thorns on his head and a wooden scepter in his left hand, the former vegetable salesman Iuri Thais, 49. He sits on a throne and declares in cathedral tones: "I am Inri Christ, the son of God, the reincarnation of Jesus, the way, the truth, and the life"[2]

For a number of years this "Inri Christ" has been touring the world. Expelled from England, he went to France. During the past few years he has set up a headquarters in Brasília.

Meanwhile, in a remote corner of Siberia, in a little village called "the House of the Dawn," a gentle man with a white tunic, long brown hair, and a timid enigmatic smile says he is the Christ, who has come back to save humanity. He doesn't tell this to everyone—only to his disciples. But there are thousands of them, and they worship him as a true god. They believe he is a reincarnation of Jesus Christ. His birth name is Sergei Torop, a former Russian soldier. He calls himself Vissarion, and says he is "the giver of new life."

Kevin Sullivan, a journalist from the United States, published in the Washington *Post* an interview with a number of Vissarion's disciples. What they told Sullivan surprised him. Lula Derbina, for example, was a translator for the International Red Cross, and she has found in Vissarion what she had been looking for all her life. "I fully believe he is Jesus Christ. I know that as surely as I know I am breathing," she stated.

Galina Oshepkova, 54, was recently divorced and the mother of two children when someone showed her a video. In it she heard Vissarion state that he had returned to earth because people had forgotten the words and teachings he left 2,000 years ago. "I felt my heart pounding and I knew: 'This is true.' He really is the one. He is the second incarnation of Christ."[3]

Jesus mentioned false christs as a sign of His return to earth, but it seems clear that He was not referring only to the ones I have just mentioned, or to the dozens of others who have appeared in the past and will certainly continue to do so in the future.

He also said there would be false prophets—people who believe that God has sent them to offer instant solutions to our problems. They make promises of miraculous healing and financial prosperity. Many of them claim that the blessings are reserved for people who have "faith" measured by the amount of money they send in. Such "prophets" have proliferated during the past few years, with new ones appearing every day. They have learned how to use radio, television, and other media to reach the masses. Some of them have built extensive financial empires.

They support their arguments by "testimonies" of people who claim they have had miracles performed for them. They even quote the Bible to affirm that "no one can do these signs that You do unless God is with him" (John 3:2). Here's what Jesus said about them: "Not everyone who says to Me, 'Lord, Lord,' will enter the kingdom of heaven; but he who does the will of My Father who is in heaven. . . . Many will say to Me on that day, 'Lord, Lord, did we not prophesy in Your name, and in Your name cast out demons, and in Your name perform many miracles?' And then I will declare to them, 'I never knew you; depart from Me, you who practice lawlessness'" (Matthew 7:21-23).

How could people who work miracles and do wonderful things in the name of Jesus not have His approval? The answer is in the text: They never did the will of the Father. Instead they acted according to their own way of doing and seeing things.

In a way, all such false prophets and people who say they are the Christ are a fulfillment of prophecy, but the matter goes beyond deluded people or those who take advantage of and benefit from the credulity and fanaticism of others. When Jesus spoke of false christs, He said that they would "show great signs and wonders, so as to mislead, if possible, even the elect" (Matthew 24:24). The elect—those who have accepted God's invitation to turn aside from lying and deception, from all that is false, and live only by the truth—would not be easily deceived by a miraculous healing or believe simply because someone says they are the reincarnation of Jesus.

If even enlightened people can be deceived, it is because the matter is much more serious than we may have thought. The key word here is "deceived." According to Jesus, during the last days there will be a deception so clever, so powerful, that it will sweep away millions. Who will be behind this deception, and how will it come about? The Bible gives us the answer.

In the book of Revelation we find that the father of lies, the master of deception in the last days, will be the same one who in the beginning swept away a third of the angels with His seduction and lies. The apostle John saw this in vision: "And the great dragon was thrown down, the serpent of old who is called the devil and Satan, who deceives the whole world; he was thrown down to the earth, and his angels were thrown down with him" (Revelation 12:9).

Note that one of the characteristics of this evil being is that he "deceives the whole world." Specializing in deception instead of force, he convinces people and makes them want to follow him. They actually believe in what he teaches and are convinced that he is right.

The strategy that he uses to persuade the multitudes to follow him voluntarily is one of seduction and lies. Jesus described the deceiver as someone who "does not stand in the truth because there is no truth in him. Whenever he speaks a lie, he speaks from his own nature, for he is a liar and the father of lies" (John 8:44).

The last battle, the one that the book of Revelation calls "Armageddon" and that will take place just before the return of Christ, will not be a conflict involving cannons or missiles. It will not be East against West, nor socialism against capitalism. The last battle of the ages will be between reality and fiction, between the truth and error, between good and evil. And its battlefield is the human heart.

The enemy is a liar by nature, and he will attempt to deceive as many as possible in the last days of history, including even the most cautious. To achieve this, of course, he will not come as he truly is. If he did that, no one would believe him. The apostle Paul says that the enemy will camouflage himself. "Even Satan disguises himself as an angel of light" (2 Corinthians 11:14). If he "disguises himself as an angel of light," that means he will be a spiritual, religious personality, a miracle worker. If not, he would never be able to trick so many people with his clever schemes.

The apostle Paul describes the way the deceiver will seek to achieve his goals: "Now we request you, brethren, with regard to the coming of our Lord Jesus Christ . . . , that you not be quickly shaken. . . . Let no one in any way deceive you, for it will not come unless the apostasy comes first, and the man of lawlessness is revealed, the son of destruction, who opposes and exalts himself above every so-called god or object of worship, so that he takes his seat in the temple of God, displaying himself as being God" (2 Thessalonians 2:1-4).

Here we have a vital key to understanding the matter. The apostle states that before the Lord Jesus returns to earth we will see this "apostasy" and the coming of the "man of sin" (verse 3, KJV). Who is the "man of sin" that he refers to? What is the "apostasy" he is talking about, and when will it happen?

Paul himself mentions other characteristics of the "man of sin." He says that he "opposes and exalts himself above every so-called god or object of worship." But he exalts himself against God in a strange way. He "opposes" without opposing. Instead of speaking against God, he disguises himself, "displaying himself as God," and "he takes his seat in the temple of God." The "man of sin" fights against God by pretending to be God. Multitudes believe him, follow him, and accept his teaching. But in doing so they naturally fall into apostasy—that is, rebellion against God.

Do you know of any religious power in our time that attributes to itself divine power? Have you ever seen a religious institution that pretends to have authority even to change what is written in the Word of God? That would be scary! The day that you witness human beings exalting themselves as God's exclusive representative, you can know that this is part of the fulfillment of Bible prophecy.

Jesus said that when the time of His return is near, we will see "the abomination of desolation which was spoken of through Daniel the prophet, standing in the holy place (let the reader understand)" (Matthew 24:15). The phrase "let the reader understand" is in parentheses. Not all will understand. It will depend on the attitude with which we search for the truth. God reveals Himself only to those who seek Him with sincerity and humility of heart.

And what is this "abomination of desolation" that the prophet Daniel talks about? To learn the answer we need to go to the book of Daniel, in which we read about a religious power that "will speak out against the Most High and wear down the saints of the Highest One, and he will intend to make alterations in times and in law" (Daniel 7:25). It says that this power "grew up to the host of heaven" and "even magnified itself to be equal with the Commander of the host. . . . And it will fling truth to the ground and perform its will and prosper" (Daniel 8:10-12).

Notice that at some point in history this religious power would attempt to change times and the law, and would "fling truth to the ground." Why such hatred for truth? Because behind this power is the father of lies. Truth and lies are like light and darkness—they don't belong together. The enemy of God would invent a false and deceitful law to get people's attention away from the true law.[4] He would do all this using his weapons of choice: deception and seduction.

"Deceive" is a key word for understanding Satan's plan. The dictionary says that it means: "To give a lie the appearance of truth. To induce someone to believe and hold to be certain what is not." As a result, deception involves leading someone into error, to direct them astray.

In Matthew 24 Jesus repeats the warning against deception four times, saying that it will be the most powerful instrument the enemy has in the last days.

The apostle Paul continues his description of the "man of sin," declaring that those who follow him will be lost because they fail to "receive the love of the truth" (2 Thessalonians 2:10). Instead, they prefer to "believe a lie" (verse 11, KJV).

At this point we need to ask: What truth is Paul talking about? What truth are they rejecting? Where do we find this truth? Jesus answered that question many centuries ago when He prayed for His disciples, saying: "Sanctify them through thy truth; thy word is truth" (John 17:17, KJV).

There are times we need to stop and think. It can be painful to confront the truth, because in the truth there exist a world of possibilities that lead toward the unknown and that inspire fear. But did you ever stop to think what would have happened if Newton hadn't been willing to learn the truth when the apple fell on his head? Or if one day Christopher Columbus had not been willing to strike out into the unknown?

The Bible tells us that in the days just before the return of Christ many people will prefer to believe error. Maybe they find it more comfortable and less painful than the truth—like the cancer patient who prefers to have the doctor tell him it isn't so, hoping that the disease will go away.

But the apostle saw even beyond that. He said that a "man of sin," or "man of lawlessness," will originate the biggest and most daring scheme ever, a masterpiece of deception: he will imitate the return of

Christ. Thus he will come, says the apostle, "in accord with the activity of Satan, with all power and signs and false wonders, and with all the deception of wickedness for those who perish, because they did not receive the love of the truth so as to be saved" (2 Thessalonians 2:8-10). Do you see that the apostle is talking about a falsification here, an imitation of the return of Christ so clever that it nearly fools even God's people?

It is interesting to notice the word "coming." It is the Greek *parousia*. Paul employs the word when he refers to the deception of the "lawless one," but it is the same word that the New Testament uses to refer to the glorious manifestation of the Lord Jesus Christ. Is this a coincidence? Of course not. The apostle chose the word intentionally, to emphasize the nearly perfect imitation of the return of Christ by this "lawless one." The evil one has planned everything with great care in his attempt to make multitudes believe that his imitation is the true second advent of Jesus.

It will be the masterpiece of satanic deception. He is preparing the world for it right now, as you read this. Observe the popular themes of the movies, literature, and electronic games that millions buy today. We live in a culture saturated with magic, with the supernatural and extraterrestrial. Children come to believe that such things are real. On the other hand, notice the paranormal phenomena carried out by spiritism. Why wouldn't people believe in an evil spirit who comes disguised as Christ and does such spectacular things?

Notice two ideas found in this text. First, this false *parousia* is "in accord with the activity of Satan." A supernatural power lies behind it. And it is evil in nature. Although it is accompanied by signs and wonders, it is still evil. John said as much when he described this satanic power in the book of Revelation: "He performs great signs, so that he even makes fire come down out of heaven to the earth in the presence of men. And he deceives those who dwell on the earth because of the signs which it was given him to perform in the presence of the beast, telling those who dwell on the earth to make an image to the beast who had the wound of the sword and has come to life" (Revelation 13:13, 14). Satanic power "deceives those who dwell on the earth." The signs and wonders convince people. They accept the deception as if it were the truth of God.

Thus signs and miracles are not necessarily evidence that God is at work. "It was given" to this evil one to do miracles. God allowed him to perform genuine miracles. As a result, human beings run the risk of being deceived and serving as instruments of evil, believing that they are doing things in Jesus' name, especially when the supernatural is present.

The second thought that comes from this verse is that such deception works with those who do not "love the truth," with those who are not fervent students of the Word of God, who are not willing to receive and obey it. Whether they do so because of fear, or because of preconceived ideas, or for whatever reason, they still have not accepted the truth found only in the Word of God.

It was because of the falsification of His coming that Jesus warned His disciples: "Then if anyone says to you, 'Behold, here is the Christ,' or 'There He is,' do not believe him. . . . If they say to you, 'Behold, He is in the wilderness,' do not go out, or, 'Behold, He is in the inner rooms,' do not believe them" (Matthew 24:23-26).

I was talking a short time ago with Armando Juárez, a Mexican writer who lives in the United States, and he said to me: "Imagine what would happen if one day a spaceship were to land at some capital of the world. All the news media would send their reporters and camera crews to cover the event. Then what if, before the eyes of the whole world, a radiant charismatic being were to step out, who claims to be Christ? Who would dare to doubt if it performs miracles that can be proved scientifically?"

The only protection against such a deception is a profound knowledge of the Word of God. Jesus said: "You will know the truth, and the truth will make you free" (John 8:32). But we live in a day when few people really care that much about knowing the truth. Ignorant of the fundamental principles of the Word of God, they have no clue as to what Scripture actually says about anything. They dedicate their effort and energy to fantasy instead of taking the time to study the Bible and understand it.

The Lord Jesus Christ told His disciples how things would be at the time of His return. He said: "For just as the lightning comes from the east and flashes even to the west, so will the coming of the Son of Man be" (Matthew 24:27).

The second coming of Jesus will be visible to everyone. The countless millions who live on our planet will see Him approaching in glory. "Every eye will see Him," wrote the apostle John (Revelation 1:7). Afterward he tried to describe in human terms what the Lord showed Him in symbolic vision: "And I saw heaven opened, and behold, a white horse, and He who sat on it is called Faithful and True" (Revelation 19:11). This mighty horseman, of course, is Jesus, and Scripture here refers to Him as the one who is "True." He is authentic and genuine. The other is an imitation—the father of lies, the deceiver.

John continues his description: "His eyes are a flame of fire, and on His head are many diadems; and He has a name written on Him which no one knows except Himself. . . . His name is called The Word of God. And the armies which are in heaven, clothed in fine linen, white and clean, were following Him on white horses. . . . And on His robe and on His thigh He has a name written, 'KING OF KINGS, AND LORD OF LORDS'" (verses 12-16).

Christ returns to put an end to the history of sin. Then there will be no more suffering, no more tears. Death will never again snatch away a loved one from our side. The sorrows and tragedies of this life will be over. "And He will wipe away every tear from their eyes; and there will no longer be any death; there shall no longer be any mourning, or crying, or pain; the first things have passed away" (Revelation 21:4).

When I was a little boy, one day I ran away from home for fear of being punished. I had done something wrong and knew that my mother would be settling accounts with me soon. So I ran and ran and ran, believing that at the infinite point of the horizon I could hide from my mistakes. Afraid to stop, I ran, not knowing where I was going. I simply ran.

The sun was setting over the wheat fields. The shadows of night mingled with my fears, imprisoning me. The distant call of the owls seemed like mocking laughter. Tired, cold, and hungry, I curled up under the eaves of an abandoned house, overcome by fatigue. I have no idea how long I slept. I only know that I woke up startled. A hand was gently brushing my face. It was my mother.

"It's OK, son," she whispered tenderly in my ears. "You ran too much. Now it's time to go back. Let's go home."

This is the most beautiful truth of all time. You, too, have run too much. You have suffered; you have wept. But Jesus says: "You've run enough, My child. Now it's time to go home. Come! I'll show you the way."

Will you accept His invitation?

The answer is yours alone.

---

[1] "Pastor With 666 Tattoo Claims to Be Divine"; www.cnn.com/2007/US/02/16/miami.preacher/.

[2] "Profetas ou malucos?"; www.terra.com.br/istoe/politica/143729.htm.

[3] "Russian Orthodoxy and Religious Pluralism: Post-Soviet Challenges"; www.cerc.unimelb.edu.au/publications/CERCWP 012003.pdf.

[4] The law given by God and written with His own finger appears in Exodus 20:3-17.

Four

Religious Skepticism and Secularism

"For even though they knew God, they did not honor Him as God or give thanks, but they became futile in their speculations, and their foolish heart was darkened. Professing to be wise, they became fools. . . . For they exchanged the truth of God for a lie, and worshiped and served the creature rather than the Creator, who is blessed forever. Amen" (Romans 1:21-25).

The sun was kissing New York City passionately that August day in 1995, sending the temperature into triple digits. I tried to cool off with an ice-cold lemonade at a bar in Rockefeller Center.

I was in the heart of Manhattan. My teacher, a Frenchman born in the United States, was having a beer. We had never spoken outside the classroom before, or discussed anything except academic subjects. Now he asked me who I was and what I did. When he heard my answer, his expression changed. Taking another slow draft of beer, he looked at me like a lost child and asked: "Is it possible to believe in God today?"

Sensing the irony in his voice, I smiled and kept on drinking my lemonade.

From then on, every time we spoke the teacher guided our conversation toward matters of religion. He claimed to have no spiritual quest. Instead, he maintained that he just wanted to prove to me that God doesn't exist. I let him talk. Listening carefully to what such individuals have to say upsets and confuses them. They get tangled in the spiderweb of their own reasoning. That's why I listen and smile.

The mind of this distinguished man, apparently successful in life, was brilliant and inquisitive. His ability to argue was outstanding. He could easily prove to anyone that it is night even if the sun is shining brightly overhead. According to his view of things, he and everything he has achieved in life are absolute proof that human beings have no need of God.

The days went by. Nothing is more effective than time for analyzing the consistency of concepts. During one of our last conversations he made a show of arguments against the existence of God. I saw no need to keep on discussing the matter, but he insisted. I began to wonder what he was really trying to accomplish. Finally when he stopped for breath, I said,

"All right, Professor, let's just imagine that you are right. There really is no God. And let's imagine too that you have a son, an only son who is 20 years old and in the flower of life. A son you love, for whom you would gladly give your life. To your sorrow, he gets addicted to drugs. You, as his father, have already done all you can to help him. You look for the best specialists, you place him in the finest rehabilitation programs, you weep, you cry out and suffer. But nothing and no one is able to do anything to help your son get free from the clutches of the vice. But you have attempted to prove to me that God does not exist. Tell me, then, where will you turn if He doesn't? What hope is there for your son?"

The man shifted nervously from one side to another on the brown sofa. His eyes seemed moist. Usually they pierced right through me. This time the eyes were sad. I could see the emotion on his face. Suffering and pain. Without realizing it, I had touched an open wound in his heart. The wound bleeds. For a moment he attempted to say something, but did not succeed. Wordless, he got up, nodded goodbye, and left. And as he departed, I saw him discreetly wipe away a tear.

The following day I learned that he did have a son. An only son—20 years old—who has been completely destroyed by drugs. Now I think I can understand his rebellion, his strange intellectual pride, even the irony of his questions.

Some weeks later, before returning to Brazil, I stopped by to take leave of my professor. He accompanied me in silence to the ground floor. There we embraced. We both knew our conversation had not yet finished. He was emotional. Words didn't come, though—they had stuck in his throat. Suddenly he swallowed and whispered in my ear.

"Pastor, you know I don't believe in God, but you do. Please, ask Him to help my boy."

I felt sorry for this distinguished scholar. It made me sad to see his eyes filled with tears, feeling helpless before the misfortune of the son he loves, and yet incapable of seeking a solution with God. He was the product of a generation of the time just before the second coming of Jesus. The apostle Paul describes it this way: "For even though they knew God, they did not honor Him as God, or give thanks; but they became futile in their speculations" (Romans 1:21).

The basic problem of people in our time is pride. They have, indeed, become "futile in their speculations." The Spanish journalist Francisco Umbral, a columnist for the newspaper *El Mundo,* illustrates the apostle's statement. Shortly before he died he wrote:

41

"Nietzsche and all the others that we know about shut the door on the old world, decreeing the death of God and the loneliness of man. This is modernity, and there is nothing to do about it. Archaic institutions, such as the church, are living today only for residual reasons."[1]

Umbral could have cited Kant, Schopenhauer, Feuerbach, Marx, or Freud to show his modernity. We shouldn't be surprised. The Bible said it a long time ago. In our current era called "postmodern" we find an abundance of such thinking. It is a general tendency, especially in the developed countries. Many intellectuals think and offer their opinions with a "pride of reasoning." Liking to be called freethinkers, they do not wish to have a commitment with anything or anyone. And even less with someone they could never see or touch, such as God.

Some are deists. They believe in a God who created and then forgot about His creation and has nothing more to do with it. Others are agnostics, who claim it's impossible to know if God exists. Finally, there are atheists, who are sure that He doesn't.

Such thinkers consider God "an outmoded, archaic, infantile concept." Attacking Him has become fashionable. Some time ago the French philosopher Michel Onfray wrote his *Atheist Manifesto*.[2] In France alone it sold 200,000 copies. Ohfray declares confidently in one passage in the book: "The last god will disappear with the last of men, and with the last of men will disappear fear, anxiety, those machines that produce divinities."

Maybe Onfray is not alone in his concepts. Richard Dawkins, the English biologist, also wrote another book of the same kind called *The God Delusion*.[3] It is a desperate effort to prove that God is nothing more than a myth that time has at last overcome. Furthermore, the British-American journalist Christopher Hitchens,[4] who lives in Washington, D.C., published *God Is Not Great,* and the North American philosopher Sam Harris recently wrote *Letter to a Christian Nation.*[5] In it Harris defends himself from the criticism that he received after his first book, in which he considered the idea of God to be ridiculous.

All these authors have something in common. For them, human beings have no need of God or of His help to be a good citizen. They say that morality does not depend on religion and that an atheist can be ethical and good. And that is all that one needs to be happy. Such individuals find support for their ideas in the neurosciences, whose "discoveries" prove that even chimpanzees have moral ideas and feel empathy and solidarity, yet "they never pray or believe in God."[6]

The point here is not whether someone who rejects God can have moral criteria or not. Morality is not the exclusive domain of Christians. The point is that Bible prophecy foretold that during the last days of earth's history such thinking would become more and more common. Today, not believing in God is almost a rule among intellectuals. One survey of scientists concludes that 60 percent of them are atheists.[7]

However, if we look at the world from a broader perspective, we will see that in spite of the skepticism of many there is an apparent awakening of human beings in favor of religiosity. For example, in Holland, often considered the most agnostic country of Europe, there has developed a surprising return to prayer.

A few years ago some Dutch Christians started what they called the Prayer in the Workplace movement. At first, hardly anyone paid any attention to it. Why should they take notice? After all, Holland was destined to become an agnostic country, and many considered prayer "an irrational although inoffensive pastime."

Nevertheless, today, "prayer in the workplace" is becoming an accepted phenomenon, with hundreds of companies taking part. Government ministries, universities, and multinational corporations (such as Philips, KLM and ABMANRO) allow their employees to organize regular prayer encounters in the workplace. Labor unions have even begun to press the government to recognize the right of employees to pray in their workplace.[8]

Adjiedj Bakas, a professional observer of trends, and Minne Buwalda, a journalist, both authors of the recent study *De Toekomst van God* (The Future of God), speak of what they call the "Dutch relapse into religiosity."[9]

Remarkable? Maybe, and maybe not. Such an apparent return of the people to prayer and spiritual praise is not necessarily a return to the Bible. Many people have concluded that agnosticism does not satisfy the deepest needs of the human heart, and they come back to the notion of religion—not to the absolute values of an absolute God, but to the relativism of a "god energy" that expects nothing and simply gives an approval to whatever behavior style that the person decides to follow. It is a sort of Christless Christianity.

The *Sunday Times* published a news report that alarmed many Christians. Church leaders of a European country wrote a prayer called "The Millennium Resolution" to mark the arrival of the year 2000. The prayer made no reference to God or to Jesus Christ.[10]

Is this Christian postmodernism? The apostle Paul mentioned such a form of Christianity as a sign of the times of the end, saying: "Holding to a form of godliness, although they have denied its power" (2 Timothy 3:5).

When Christianity takes the name of Christ but does not live by His teachings, it loses its authority. Some non-Christian Europeans do not accept Christianity, because they see the state of corruption of its spiritual leaders. According to participants in an encounter organized by Catholic laypeople called Operation Mobilization, non-Christians are shocked by the delinquency, prostitution, and pornography so common in the Christian world. Monica Maggio, a Christian volunteer, states that non-Christians are dismayed at the chaos of Western society. As a result, Christians, because of their religious deterioration, are in no condition to help them.[11]

A study in Germany concluded that 20 percent of the people who consider themselves Protestants and 10 percent of Catholics are, in fact, deists. They believe in God, but that does not interfere with their lives. According to the German magazine *Der Spiegel,* the Christian church of Germany has fallen largely into irrelevance. Christian values are having less and less impact on society today. According to a recent survey, only 37 percent of the German population considers that the church imparts moral values. The German public regard the police, the political parties, and the environmental organization Greenpeace as better qualified than churches to promote values.[12]

The truth is that human beings have determined in their hearts not to believe in God anymore, or they believe in Him only as a sort of depersonalized energy, a force, or simply an insignificant being that they can manage to their liking. They have shoved the sovereign and all-powerful Creator-God off the stage of their existence.

In spite of modern humanity's defiant attitude, God, far from dying, as Nietzsche predicted would happen, is still in control of life and of the universe. But as for those who deny His existence, the only thing they have left is "the loneliness of man," to use the philosopher's own words. And what kind of man? One sinking every day more and more in the quicksand of his rationality. "For even though they knew God, they did not honor Him as God or give thanks, but they became futile in their speculations. . . . Professing to be wise, they became fools" (Romans 1:21, 22), wrote the apostle Paul more than 2,000 years ago.

Let's for a moment return to my agnostic teacher. Among the arguments he used to prove that the personal God that Christians worship does not exist was the supposed presence of cosmic energy that permeates everything in space or on earth. In reality he believed in God but preferred to call Him "energy." My teacher wore a gold chain around his neck. On the end of the chain was a tiny crystal pyramid. According to him, it would attract the cosmic energy of the universe. The Bible described this kind of thinking many centuries ago when it said: "They exchanged the truth of God for a lie, and worshiped and served the creature rather than the Creator" (verse 25).

My teacher had an inquiring mind and was a professor in a famous school for executives in Manhattan. But instead of worshiping the Creator, he was honoring something that the true God had created. The man focused his attention on a crystal. When things began going badly, he would take the stone and concentrate on it, almost with an attitude of devotion, to receive "energy rays." He believed this was much wiser and more intelligent that praying to God.

Unfortunately, such behavior is not unusual in our day. Humanity has shifted its attention from the Creator to what He has made. Some people will not go out of their house without consulting their horoscope. They believe that the stars—objects created by God—actually determine their destiny.

Eighty years ago astrologist Llewellyn George stated something that no one then took seriously. "The time has arrived," he wrote, "for the masses as a whole to take an interest in [astrology]."[13]

Said at a time that people were fascinated by the birth of technology and scientific discovery, his words didn't seem to make much sense. But today, when we see millions of human beings with their attention directed to the stars, we realize that he was not mistaken.

Why are people seeking their destiny in astrology? Because they have a deep spiritual need of the soul, an inward emptiness, a lack of sense in a life that does not look beyond material values. People may be unaware of that need, but it is there in everything they do. Under such circumstances astrology can assume an important role. It appears to make sense of otherwise inexplicable parts of your personality. Offering advice about money, friendship, or love, it demands nothing in return in the area of moral conduct. People like that. We want to decide what is right or wrong for ourselves without outside interference. The eternal principles of God have no relevance for many. The only thing that matters is information that will help them manage in whatever way they want. They will not allow anyone to tell them what they ought to do.

At first such a perspective may seem comforting, but it does not satisfy the spiritual hunger of the soul. Religion will always fail to meet the existential questions of life if it draws aside from the only Book capable of giving satisfactory answers. When we use the Bible, but accommodate it to our own wishes; when we pick and choose what fits our lifestyle and way of thinking, but refuse to conform our lifestyle to the eternal teaching of the Word of God, then it is worth nothing.

Astrology takes advantage of such emptiness. Nothing more than a supposed science blended with esoteric ideas, it is based on a series of ancient concepts that believed in the influence of the stars in human destiny. Priests and other specialists employed it to announce the most propitious times for planting and harvesting and other activities. Kings had their private astrologers who told them the best time to go to war or refrain from war. The practice passed from one generation to another, and as time went on it got more sophisticated, until our day.

The astrologer Margaret Hone attempts to explain her belief, saying: "Astrology is a particular system of interpretation of the relationship that exists between planetary action and human experience."[14] From the astrologers' point of view, such "planetary influences" determine the behavior or attitudes of human beings. That is, they attempt to give scientific base to human speculations; but astrology is not the same as astronomy. In reality, behind the astrological interpretations lurk the gods of ancient mythologies. The astrologists attribute to the planets characteristics derived from the old polytheism. But the face that astrology shows people is that of the stars and not of the gods. And many people follow it, believing that they are dealing with "science."[15]

Today astrology permeates in one way or another many human activities. And it shows up in other esoteric and mystical disciplines. Some people believe that human destiny depends on magic numbers, precious stones, or even colors. Multitudes hope to find in such concepts the solution to their problems.

Surveys indicate that 95 percent of the people in the United States believe in astrology, flying saucers, ghosts, crystals, or some other type of superstition. The United States alone has more than 10,000 astrologists and people who read tarot cards. Their clients include many famous people. The interest in such matters is so huge than an organization established by the late guru Maharashi Mahesh Yogi has earned $3 million.[16]

What is behind the fascination with such topics? No doubt it is the same being who, according to the Bible account, one day came to the first woman, Eve, and made her believe that a special power resided in the fruit that he offered her. You and I know that that the fruit did not have the magical properties he claimed for it. The serpent's goal was not just to get the woman to eat the forbidden fruit, but to draw her away from her Creator and lead her to pay attention to created things. Satan uses the supposed power of divining for only one purpose—to deceive.

The Word of God is categorical on the matter: "When they say to you, 'Consult the mediums and the spiritists who whisper and mutter,' should not a people consult their God? Should they consult the dead on behalf of the living?" (Isaiah 8:19).

Christianity should be the strongest bastion of Bible values, but some Christians instead follow deceptive religious theories born in the mind of the evil one. Such doctrines have no basis in the Bible.

One example is the prevalent belief in the immortality of the soul. The Bible clearly states that the person who dies knows nothing until the resurrection. "For the living know they will die; but the dead do not know anything, nor have they any longer a reward, for their memory is forgotten. Indeed their love, their hate and their zeal have already perished, and they will no longer have a share in all that is done under the sun" (Ecclesiastes 9:5, 6).

If the dead "will no longer have a share in all that is done under the sun," how can the spirits of the dead come back? How can anyone converse with them? Scripture continues: "Whatever your hand finds to do, do it with all your might; for there is no activity or planning or knowledge or wisdom in Sheol [the grave] where you are going" (verse 10).

If the grave—that is, death—has no place for anything more, how can anyone be reincarnated into other life forms? Where does this idea come from? Evidently from a deceitful power—from the devil—just as is revealed in Scripture. What he wants to do is confuse people. Notice that in recent times those who claim to be Christ call themselves the *reincarnation* of Jesus. Isn't that interesting? Do you think it's a coincidence? Or is there a master plan behind it all?

This is a serious matter. Christians must take the Word of God as their only rule of faith and doctrine. They must not accept spurious teachings. Nor dare they trust in the authority of a church or the force of tradition. That can be fatal when spiritual matters are at stake.

If Christians lay aside the Word of God and trust in human concepts, they are destroying the foundation of their faith. The result is the secularization of Christianity. The word "secular" has its origin in the Latin word *secularis,* meaning something related to the present state of things, to contemporary culture and values. Humanity in our time lives under the influence of scientific and technological experience. Both emphasize the importance of matter and end up as materialistic philosophies. Christians are not immune to the influence of such ways of thinking, and the result is a secularized Christianity.

Secularized Christians believe in God, but God becomes simply a name, a detail of history, useful, perhaps, as a sort of amulet for when they get in a pinch. But when the danger is past, they feel no more obligation toward Him. They live most of their lives as if God didn't exist at all.

The only difference between pagans and secularized Christians is that the latter go to church once in a while. They are, so to speak, members of a religious club. When they do go to church, it is not so much to worship God as to observe the program with a typical consumer's mind-set. If they like the product, they come back. But if not, they criticize it and look for another church that satisfies their expectations. After all, they are "paying" with their offerings and expect to receive in exchange a top-quality product.

Religious leaders find themselves forced to scramble to find a new "product" to attract the "spectators." In a competitive world they must make every effort to have the best show in town. If necessary, they are willing to lower the standards of Bible principles and say that God offers only love, never punishment or retribution. The amazing grace of Christ covers any and all human deficiency, including the lives of people who do not acknowledge or abandon their sins.

Paul spoke of the sad result of such an attitude: "And just as they did not see fit to acknowledge God any longer, God gave them over to a depraved mind, to do those things which are not proper" (Romans 1:28).

What are those "things which are not proper"? Writing to his disciple Timothy, Paul explains: "But realize this, that in the last days difficult times will come. For men will be lovers of self, lovers of money, boastful, arrogant, revilers, disobedient to parents, ungrateful, unholy, unloving, irreconcilable, malicious gossips, without self-control, brutal, haters of good, treacherous, reckless, conceited, lovers of pleasure rather than lovers of God" (2 Timothy 3:1-4).

People who take God out of their lives end up,

sooner or later, removing the barriers to sin. "It's eternal as long as it lasts," they repeat to themselves again and again. They attempt to justify a lifestyle whose only purpose is to gratify their senses. But unable ever to achieve it, they feel empty and incomplete. Wanting to find happiness at any price, they struggle in vain to get it—and miss it every time.

The Bible calls this terrible frustration "sin." In Scripture the word translated "sin" comes from the Greek expression *hamartia,* which means, literally, to miss the mark, to aim at one thing and hit another. Seeking to pursue happiness, they end up unhappy, badly confused, and lost. But modern people insist on trying to ignore sin. In fact, the word itself is completely out of style. Instead, some call it "inner imbalance," "human fragility," "deviant conduct," "personal preference"—anything but sin. As if changing the name could solve the problem.

I heard about a campaign that a teacher organized in a school asking the children to give ideas about how to solve the energy crisis. "The world's fuel supply is about gone," she told them, "and we need suggestions to keep it from happening."

The next day the children came with some amazing ideas:

"Tie a dog beside each driver and teach it to bark if he goes too fast. That way he won't burn up so much gas," one child said.

"Stop selling gasoline," another proposed. "Then it won't run out."

But the most interesting idea came from a boy who said: "Let's change the name of gasoline. Then people will buy something else, and gasoline will be safe."

That seems to the solution of many in our time who think that they have found a way around the sin problem by staying far away from God. But if human beings came originally from the hand of God, they can be fulfilled and complete only when they return to their Creator.

Yet people try to deny reality. They forget that they are children of God and should live as such. From childhood their worldview has been distorted. God is something without much relevance or importance. On television they watch programs that make fun of spiritual things. Then they grow up accepting the secularized life as something normal.

In the late 1980s someone discovered what the press called a "monkey child" in the jungles of Uganda. This human child had evidently lived with a tribe of apes for at least four or five years. The authorities took the boy, who appeared to be about 6 years old, to a hospital and later to an orphanage, where he hopped and moved in circles like a chimpanzee. He refused to eat the food that they offered, and bit anyone who approached him.[17]

The experts who studied the boy's behavior said that if a child lives with animals for more than four or five years, it is nearly impossible for him or her to return to normal behavior afterward. The brain receives indelible marks that will last for the rest of the child's life.

Something like that seems to have happened to human beings today. Living in a world of rationalism, they have forgotten that they came from the hand of God. They reap the consequences of existing separated from the Creator. The sad results include broken families and children enslaved to the world of drugs and promiscuity. That is the sad and desperate reality that people endure every hour, every minute. They suffer, lose their will to live, and then in desperation invent stopgap measures to ease the pain and still the cry of anguish from their hearts.

Why do you continue to endure in silence the pain that no one sees? In the darkest hour of your life, when the pain takes away your will to live, when you look for an answer from inside yourself and find none, why don't you decide to return to your Creator?

More than 2,000 years ago the Lord Jesus looked at the spiritual panorama of our day and asked: "When the Son of Man comes, will He find faith on the earth?" (Luke 18:8). What He wonders is if people will still remember that He loves them and waits for them with open arms. Will you remember?

The answer is yours alone.

―――――――

[1] Francisco Umbral, in *El Mundo* (Spain), Oct. 6, 1996.

[2] Michel Onfray, *Tratado de Ateología* (Buenos Aires: Editora Argentina, 2005).

[3] Richard Dawkins, *The God Delusion* (Boston: Mariner Book Company, 2006).

[4] Christopher Hitchens, *God Is Not Great: How Religion Poisons Everything* (New York: Hachette Book Group, 2007).

[5] Sam Harris, *Letter to a Christian Nation* (New York: Vintage Books, 2007).

[6] "Neurociencia"; www.nce.ufrj.br/ginape/publicacoes/trabalhos/RenatoMaterial/neurociencia.htm.

[7] L. G. Quevedo, "O neo-ateísmo"; www.miradaglobal.com/index.php?option=com_content&task=view&id=737&Itemid=9&lang=pt.

[8] Philip Jenkins, *God's Continent: Christianity, Islam, and Europe's Religious Crisis.*

[9] Discussed in Joshua Livestro, "Holland's Post-Secular Future"; www.weeklystandard.com/Utilities/printer_preview.asp?idArticle=13110&R=EF26165.10 *Sunday Times*, Dec. 31, 1999.

[11] "Operación movilización"; www.mnnonline.org/es/article/9582.

[12] *Der Spiegel,* No. 13, 2006.

[13] Llewellyn George, *A to Z Horoscope Maker and Delineator,* 10th ed. (St. Paul, Minn.: Llewellyn Worldwide, Ltd., 2003), p. 18.

[14] Margaret E. Hone, *The Modern Textbook of Astrology* (London: L. N. Fowler and Com., Ltd., 1951), p. 10.

[15] Charles Strohmer, *What Your Horoscope Doesn't Tell You* (Wheaton, Ill.: Tyndale Pub. House), p. 25.

[16] José Cutileiro, "Maharishi Mahesh Yogi"; http://aeiou.expresso.pt/gen.pl?p=stories&op=view&fokey=ex.stories/244986.

[17] http://expedienteoculto.blogspot.com/2007/06/los-nios-salvajes.html.

Five

Earthquakes and Hurricanes

*"There will be signs in sun and moon and stars, and on the earth
dismay among nations, in perplexity at the roaring of the sea
and the waves, men fainting from fear and the expectation
of the things which are coming upon the world; for the powers of
the heavens will be shaken" (Luke 21:25, 26).*

Eleven-year-old Ismael Gumuda weeps his tragedy.
Sorry to be alive, he would have preferred to be dead
and feel nothing. Every time he remembers his brother,
he cries again. How can he ever get the images out of his
mind? By day he sees them constantly. At night they return as nightmares. He can't forget the day that the gigantic wave tore his 7-year-old brother from his arms.

They were at school, practicing their part in the
upcoming New Year's celebration, when they heard
the terrible roar of a thousand thunders. That noise
marked the end of his life forever. "We turned around
and saw the giant wave, higher than the school building, crashing on us," he says, wiping away his tears. "I
grabbed my brother and held him as tight as I could,
but a wave separated us. There was nothing I could do
to help him. He looked at me terrified, wanting me to
help, but I couldn't. The water was stronger than I was.
I survived only because the wave carried me and set
me down at the foot of the mountain. But my brother
disappeared; he was swallowed up by the sea. I miss
him a lot and I pray for him."

The teachers at the school at which he studies

have noticed that Ismael is not the same since the tsunami. He has lost weight, and he is always remote and quiet. Ismael is one of the students at Ban Tlaynork who took part in a program of psychological rehabilitation sponsored by UNICEF in Thailand.[1]

The early-morning hours of December 26, 2004, will remain forever in the memory of those who experienced its horror. Even though the years may go by, they will continue to feel shaken and perplexed.

Until that day many people had never heard of a tsunami. Suddenly, now everyone is aware of a frightening reality. What name can you give to a destructive force that, in a fraction of a second, tore away islands, made cities disappear, and ended approximately 200,000 lives? Where could anyone run to find shelter from a force that was equivalent to the explosion of a million atomic bombs like the one that destroyed Hiroshima during World War II?[2]

That morning of horror shook the planet to its foundations. The killer blow, a seaquake measuring 9.0 on the Richter scale, set in motion wave action that started in the extreme northern point of Indonesia and swept along the coasts of Thailand, India, Bangladesh, and Sri Lanka. It killed hundreds of people on the east coast of Africa and then sent huge waves crashing onto the shores of Chile in South America.

People understood, in a tragic way, how small they are when faced with the fury of nature.

The trauma experienced by the world as 2004 came to its close was only a foretaste of a 2005 filled with natural disasters. Weeks after the tsunami of Indonesia a series of hurricanes brought floods and death to Central America and the United States. Hurricane Katrina caused extensive damage and left the U.S. city of New Orleans under water for weeks. Sludge reeking of death replaced the famous French ambience of the city considered the home of blues and jazz.[3]

In October of that same year another gigantic earthquake shook Pakistan and India, killing thousands, wounding tens of thousands, and leaving millions of people without shelter.[4] Mudslides and floods made worse by Hurricane Stan would kill hundreds in Guatemala, and the Ilamatepec Volcano in El Salvador would erupt, leading to still more deaths. Thousands of families had to evacuate.[5]

According to the Center for Research on the Epidemiology of Disasters (CRED), affiliated with the World Health Organization, just from January to October of 2005 almost 100,000 people perished from natural disasters. At its headquarters in Belgium, CRED maintains a database of world disasters. According to the organization, the number of disasters recorded has increased notably since 1900.[6]

The year 2005 could have passed into history as having the greatest number of natural disasters. But the next year recorded even more natural cataclysms. To complete the somber picture, Markka Niskala, former secretary general of the International Red Cross, stated that 2007 had 20 percent more catastrophes than 2006. Researchers currently calculate that disasters affect 250 million people every 10 years. In half of these cases the element of destruction is water.

Water is life. If there is not enough, life ceases. But too much can kill. The worst water-related disaster took place on the Yellow and Yangtze rivers in China. It killed about 4 million people. According to the Intergovernmental Panel on Climate Change, "it is probable that extreme meteorological episodes will increase in frequency and strength during the twenty-first century due to climate changes."[7]

Faced with this reality, people everywhere are asking: What is happening to our planet? Has it gone mad? When will all of this end? The answers are even more macabre. Many religious people are preaching divine wrath and destruction of the world. The astrologists are blaming the influence of the stars, while the scientific community attributes everything to global warming provoked by human mismanagement of the earth and its resources.

"Global warming" is a relatively new expression. Science uses it to explain the earth's increase in average annual temperature. Nobody questions that the earth has become warmer in recent decades. Specifically, the process began at the start of the Industrial Revolution, when society gave more importance to productivity than to quality of human life.

Gases, released by factories, motor vehicles, forest fires, and other industrial and personal activity, have been both destroying the protective ozone layer and creating a "greenhouse" effect that traps more of the heat from the sun's rays. As a result, the earth's temperature is increasing, glaciers are melting, and the sea level is rising.[8]

Since 1961 the sea level has crept up at a rate of one to two millimeters per year.[9] The IPCC calculates that if the temperature continues to rise at the same rate that it has in recent decades, the sea level could be up as much as 140 centimeters by the end of the century.[10]

Eight of the warmest years on record have been recorded since 1998.[11] The Northern Hemisphere has about 5 percent less average snowfall than in 1966.[12]

As a child I sometimes traveled from Lima to Jauja, the city where I was born. The journey involves one of the highest rail lines in the world. The blankets of snow covering the distant peaks always fascinated me. Perpetual snows covered the summits of the beautiful Ticlio range of the Andes. But the last time I was in that part of the Andes I felt heartsick to see the hills barren. Nature seemed to be dying. I heard a sad moaning caused by the cold wind that blew over the mountains. And I thought to myself, *The scientific reports we have been hearing are real.* Some assume that the changes won't affect us, because we are far from such places. But the transformations are rapidly spreading.

It is undeniable that the planet is warmer now and that humans are partly to blame. The scientific community believes that, at this point, further increase in temperature is inevitable. The sea level will continue to rise at least during the present century even if tomorrow we could completely eliminate the emission of the gases causing the greenhouse effect.

As it has become aware of the danger, the world has turned its attention to the environment. Ecology has become a sort of religion. In schools everywhere—from kindergarten to the university—students are learning about taking better care of the planet. But things don't seem to be improving. In fact, the Bible says they will grow worse and worse, and that fact is one of the signs announcing the coming of Jesus.

Al Gore, former candidate for president of the United States, received the Nobel Peace Prize in 2007 for his documentary film *Earth in the Balance,* regarded by the Nobel committee as an effort "to build up and disseminate greater knowledge about man-made climate change."[13] The film shows the human concern for saving the planet, but it also reminds us of humanity's inability to see what is really about to happen.

Sami Sobaki, director of the Max Planck Institute for Solar System Research located near Göttingen, Germany, says that in the past 60 years, in addition to the human tampering with the environment, for unexplainable reasons the sun itself has gotten hotter, contributing to the warming of the climate and consequent increase in natural disasters.[14]

Unexplainable reasons? Jesus said it many centuries ago: *"There will be signs in sun and moon and stars, and on the earth dismay among nations, in perplexity at the roaring of the sea and the waves, men fainting from fear and the expectation of the things which are coming upon the world; for the powers of the heavens will be shaken"* (Luke 21:25, 26). Doesn't that sound like a description of our day? There really is "dismay among nations," and "perplexity at the roaring of the sea."

And yet we need to be careful and not confuse things. The fact that we see such natural disasters does not mean that God is causing them. He explains the nature of His relationship with the human race. "'For I know the plans that I have for you,' declares the Lord, 'plans for welfare and not for calamity to give you a future and a hope'" (Jeremiah 29:11).

That is good news. God will not allow humanity to destroy itself. Because He loves us, He will intervene in history and put an end to human mistakes and errors. Doesn't that tell us that the glorious coming of Christ awaits us just over the horizon?

We have no need to fear. The love of God can fill our hearts with hope. The Christian hope is assurance, certainty, and confidence even when from a human perspective there appears no way out.

Many years ago, when my little son was 6 years old, he was lost in a city of more than 2 million inhabitants. My wife and I ran frantically from place to place, trying to find him. Having only recently arrived in Brazil and not very familiar with Portuguese, we wept in desperation. What to do? Where to turn? The child had totally disappeared. To find him in the midst of so many people would be something like finding a needle in a haystack.

Seeing our desperation, a guard told us: "The police are looking for your child. If he is still in the downtown area, they will find him when the businesses close."

And so it was. At 6:00 that evening the number of people in the center of the city began to diminish. Employees returned home after a long day of work. The streets began to be more deserted, and the shadows of the night began to fall on the city like a black sheet. A cold June wind began to blow.

We continued to look, and to our great joy, we found him. There he was, seated on an abandoned box, playing with a stone, unaware of the suffering of his parents. Weeping, we embraced him and covered him with kisses.

Later I asked him: "Weren't you afraid?"

"Afraid? Why?" he asked innocently.

"When children get lost, they are afraid," I told him.

He opened his eyes with surprise. "I wasn't lost, Daddy. I was just waiting. Weren't you going to look for me?"

Look around you. Do you see the darkness closing in because of natural disasters? Earthquakes, hurricanes, and tornadoes are spreading fear. The forecasts of science are terrifying. Even in the midst of such fearful expectation and dark omens I want you to know that Jesus will be arriving soon, and that He is coming to look for you. There is hope. The eternal morning is already starting to dawn. As the day grows brighter, read the promise that God has given: "When you pass through the waters, I will be with you; and through the rivers, they will not overflow you. When you walk through the fire, you will not be scorched, nor will the flame burn you" (Isaiah 43:2).

The answer is yours alone.

---

[1] www.unicef.org/emerg/disasterinasia/index_main.html.

[2] VEJA Journal, Jan. 5, 2005.

[3] http://en.wikipedia.org/wiki/Hurricane_Katrina.

[4] *USA Today,* Oct. 8, 2005.

[5] http://earthobservatory.nasa.gov/NaturalHazards/natural_hazards_v2. php3?img_id=13187.

[6] Center for Research on the Epidemiology of Disasters; www.cred.be/.

[7] www.portalplanetasedna.com.ar/desastres03.htm.

[8] "Ciencia," *Terra Notícias,* Dec. 27, 2007.

[9] http://en.wikipedia.org/wiki/Global_warming; http://en.wikipedia.org/wiki/Sea_level_rise.

[10] http://news.softpedia.com/news/Ocean-Level-May-Rise-Up-to-140-cm-by-2100-42982.shtml.

[11] www.sciencedaily.com/releases/2008/01/080116/14150.htm.

[12] http://maps.grida.no/go/searchFree/q/%22cryosphere%22%20OR%20%22snow%22%20%22snow%20cover2220OR%20snow20extent22.

[13] www.cnn.com/2007/POLITICS/10/12/nobel.gore/index.html.

[14] Michael Leidig, "Hotter-burning Sun Warming the Planet," Washington *Times,* July 19, 2004; www.freerepublic.com/focus/f-news/117456/posts.

Six

A Heartless Society

*"But realize this, that in the last days difficult times will come.
For men will be . . . disobedient to parents, ungrateful, unholy,
unloving, irreconcilable, malicious gossips, without self-control,
brutal, haters of good" (2 Timothy 3:1-3). "For many others,
the overwhelming spread of evil will do them in—nothing left . . .
but a mound of ashes" (Matthew 24:12, Message).*

Scene one. Midnight. The couple is resting, unaware of any danger. A young woman enters their room on tiptoes and checks to make sure the owners of the house are asleep. Then she shuts off the alarm system and turns on the light of the outside passageway to make it easier for two young men to enter. As they come in, the young woman looks for plastic gloves to protect their hands and panty hose to hide their faces. Minutes later the men slip into the bedroom and beat the husband and wife to death. The girl watches calmly. After the couple are dead, she and one of the young men, who is her boyfriend, go to a motel to celebrate.

At 3:00 in the morning the oldest daughter of the murdered couple arrives at home. She has been out, and before going home, she stops to pick up her little brother, who has been at an electronic game room. When they get home, they confront the scene of horror and blood. The daughter loses control and curses the people who have done such a horrendous deed. At the funeral in the cemetery she weeps hysterically, and someone has to catch her as she starts to faint.

Some days later the police arrest the murderers.

They confess and reveal that the one who thought up their evil plan and helped them carry it out was the very daughter of the murdered couple. Yes, the girl who at the cemetery wept so bitterly the day her parents were buried![1]

What could happen in the mind of an 18-year-old girl that would lead her to commit such a horrifying act? How can anyone explain it? Nevertheless, the Bible says that in the last days people will be "contemptuous of parents, crude, coarse, dog-eat-dog, unbending" (2 Timothy 3:2, 3, Message).

Scene two. While the whole world awakens from the nightmare and together turns its attention to the people affected by the devastating tsunami of 2004, the police discover an organized group who look for orphan children to use in prostitution or to remove their organs to sell them.[2] Human hyenas taking advantage of the suffering of others to benefit themselves? But again, it is the truth.

One day as I had lunch with a friend we discussed the incident. His eyes filled with tears, and almost instinctively he said to me, "I'd kill those savages. They are animals and don't deserve to live."

An instant later he blushed and said, "Sorry; I forgot that I am a Christian. Of course, I should never think like that."

Without realizing it, he was fulfilling another prophecy of the last days. Jesus said: "Because lawlessness is increased, most people's love will grow cold" (Matthew 24:12).

Scene three. A harmless city in the interior. The night is darker than usual. It is pouring rain. Joaquin and his wife are returning home from a wedding. Having been the godparents at it and still wearing their good clothes, they happily remember their own wedding. The years have passed, and they are more in love than ever. God has given them two children. That night the children are home with a babysitter. Then something unexpected interrupts the husband and wife's animated conversation. By the side of the road they see a couple in trouble. Apparently their vehicle has broken down. In spite of the rain Joaquin and his wife decide to help. A terrible mistake. A few minutes later he is dead, his face disfigured by a shotgun blast. The wife has been raped and at the point of death. It will take her years to recover, and the two little children, robbed of their father at an early age, never can understand how death could be the reward for an act of kindness. Would you have the courage to stop along the highway to help someone after hearing such a story?

We live in dangerous times. The apostle Paul said that in the last days people would be "brutal, haters of good, treacherous, reckless, conceited" (2 Timothy 3:3, 4). Everyone would be afraid of everyone else. No one would trust anyone. Gangs on every corner would fill cities of every size. The strong would take advantage of the weak.

Today large cities have turned into jungles in which the wild beasts are the humans who live there. The love of many has, indeed, grown cold. Perhaps you see on the street corner a child with disabilities begging, and a short distance away you spot those who exploit the child, waiting for their daily earnings. Feeling mocked and wounded in your heart, you decide never again to let anyone play you for a fool.

The doorbell rings, and you answer the door. A tired woman with a child in her arms asks for a glass of water. Your heart moved to help, you go to the kitchen to get the water. When you return, the woman has vanished—taking with her the laptop computer that was in your living room.

Do you still feel like helping? Your Christian spirit motivates you to continue despite the frustrations and the deception, but the majority of people today will think long and hard before they aid others. The love of many has grown cold. Jesus said it would. Evil will increase more and more as people who care will be fewer and fewer.

Why do people do such things? Not even they understand why. They know only that they are seeking for something, and in their headlong race to find it they hurt and wound others, even if the "others" are the people they love most.

The day I wrote this page the police, tipped off by an informer, knocked down the door of an apartment located in the most expensive part of a great city and found a scene that would disturb even the hardest heart. A 12-year-old girl had been tied up in the servants' quarters. As she hung by her arms from an iron stairway, her feet almost didn't touch the floor. A piece of gauze soaked in pepper covered her mouth, and eight of her fingers had been broken. Most of her nails had been torn out. "I began to shake so much that I could hardly untie her," said a police officer accustomed to seeing scenes of horror. What makes the in-

cident especially barbaric was that the one responsible
was the child's adoptive mother.[3]

Every day, in every country, one encounters violence and abuse—even in one's own home.

Alan Weisman, in his new book *The World
Without Us,*[4] imagines how our planet would be
without people. Some might think that it would be
better off, but I personally don't think so. I believe
that the real problem is that the human race is lost
in the shadows of its distance from God. There is no
other explanation.

One early Thursday morning in June, Sirlei, a
poor and struggling domestic employee who lived on
a salary of $200 per month, was waiting for the bus
that would take her to a medical appointment.
Needing to arrive in time to get a place in line, she
kept glancing impatiently at the clock. The bus was
late. A short distance away the waves were breaking
noisily against the beach. Sirlei kept thinking about
her 3-year-old son at home. He was the reason for her
every effort.

Suddenly a blow to her neck knocked her down.
Next she felt a kick in her face. Instinctively she tried
to protect herself with her arms, but it was useless. A
rain of blows and kicks showered her from all sides.
Her maternal instinct instantly made her think of her
child. She couldn't understand what was happening.
No one could. Even today society struggles to understand why five middle-class university students felt
pleasure in mutilating a defenseless woman.

The police caught them later. Their parents argued
that they were just having fun. Sirlei escaped death only

because a prostitute, who happened to be out at that time of the morning, began to scream for help.[5]

What is it that people are looking for and can't find? Human beings today seem permanently hopeless and desperate. They may deny it, argue, discuss, cry out that it's not true, but they are dissatisfied. No matter what they get, it's not enough. Lost in the tangled webs of their own desires, they slide into chaos that may destroy not only themselves but others.

Every year addicts consume $150 billion worth of illegal drugs. It is one of the most profitable businesses in the world after oil. If we were add to this the $104 billion spent on tobacco and the $525 billion on alcohol, we would understand the complete inversion of values in our society.[6]

Some believe we need to consider the legalization of drugs in order to overturn the police corruption and other crimes associated with its traffic and consumption.[7]

When Jesus mentioned this kind of wickedness as a sign of the last days, He was not predestining people to be this way. He was simply describing the reality He could foresee. The teenagers who attacked the young mother in the incident just mentioned chose to behave the way they did. They of their own free will decided to be violent and treat a fellow human being worse than an animal. No motive can ever justify their act. They weren't trying to rob her—they had money. One of them had just spent six months in Australia practicing surfing on the pretext of learning English.

A sociologist tried to explain their behavior as a product of the present-day culture of impunity. But the truth is something else. The prophet Jeremiah wrote: "The heart is more deceitful than all else and is desperately sick; who can understand it?" (Jeremiah 17:9).

The problem with human beings is their twisted and evil heart. Violent by nature, it is evil, deceitful, untrustworthy, perverse, and cruel. Education can teach people how to disguise their evil intentions, but it can never transform their hearts. They will still be dishonest and selfish no matter how sophisticated they become. For example, those who present passionate speeches in favor of peace may at the same time actively promote war. Five of the countries that earn the most from the sale of arms are on the U.N. Security Council.[8]

Only Jesus can transform the heart. He doesn't work from the outside. His transformation begins deep inside, reaching the roots of human behavior. "And I shall give them one heart, and put a new spirit within them. And I shall take the heart of stone out of their flesh and give them a heart of flesh" (Ezekiel 11:19).

I have seen the transformation that Jesus can bring to the lives of people who accept Him as their personal Savior. Nothing is impossible for Jesus. There is no one who cannot be helped and turned around.

One day He came to Bethany and found that His friend Lazarus had been dead for four days. His friend's flesh had already started to decompose. No one could imagine a remedy for a problem like that. Science can do nothing and money is useless. So is technology and everything else. But Jesus came, and when He did, life came too, because He is life.

When Jesus said, "Lazarus, come forth!" the dead

man sprang back to life. I have seen Jesus do the same miracle today. I see it every day in the countries in which I conduct evangelistic crusades. People who were spiritually dead come back to life, destroyed homes are made new, and broken dreams are converted into reality. Jesus is life, and wherever He comes in, there is fullness of life.

I met Andrés in one of the most violent cities of the world. He had spent years in prison paying for his crimes. But Jesus found him there. One cold winter night Andrés was dying. Shaking violently with cold, nearly frozen, he expected to die. It was in that condition that he heard me on the radio of a cellmate. That night the Spirit of God touched his heart. Although he had heard about Jesus many times, he thought religion was for weaklings and had always considered himself to be tough. Heartless and cruel, he had chosen a life of crime when he was scarcely an adolescent, and he blamed society for not having given him any alternative.

That night he felt himself a few minutes from death, and the thought terrified him. Yet in the dark shadows of that night he began to understand that God loved him and wanted to give him a new heart. After crying out to Jesus for a second chance, he fell asleep.

The next morning the sun streamed in his window, breaking through the clouds in spite of a thick fog. He was in the sick ward of the prison.

"I was alive," he told me, unable to hide his emotions. "I hadn't died. God was giving me a second chance."

It has been 30 years since that cold night in the freezing prison cell. Andrés is today a living testimony of the transforming power of Christ. Now free, he is doing an outstanding work for a nongovernmental organization dedicated to reaching delinquent children and youth.

The marvelous Christ who touched the life of Andrés as he was dying can also enter into your heart if you will let Him. Read what Jesus says to you: "Come to Me, all who are weary and heavy-laden, and I will give you rest" (Matthew 11:28).

Life without Christ is, indeed, a heavy burden. The weariness of spirit that some people call depression has become the illness that destroys many lives without killing the bodies. In the last days we have given it a more sophisticated name, but it is still the weariness of being alive. But Jesus urges: "Come to Me." He wants to give you rest and peace. Isn't that what you've been longing for?

The answer is yours alone.

---

[1] "Verdades e mentiras de Suzane Von Richthofen," *Revista VEJA,* Apr. 12, 2006.

[2] *Revista VEJA,* Jan. 5, 2005.

[3] "Como alguém é capaz de fazer isso?" *Revista VEJA,* Mar. 26, 2008.

[4] Alan Weisman, *The World Without Us* (New York: St. Martin's Press, 2000).

[5] "Socos, pontapés . . . ," *Revista VEJA,* July 4, 2007.

[6] Patrícia Costa, "Drogas: combater ou legalizar?" www.senac.br/informativo/diga/39/segundamateria-39.pdf.

[7] Eliot Spitzer, "The Fall of Ethics Man," *The Economist,* Mar. 11, 2008.

[8] Juan Carlos Casté, "Conferencia mundial sobre alimentación," Roma 1974; www.catolicismo.com.br/.

Seven

A Sex-obsessed Generation

*"God gave them over to degrading passions; for their women
exchanged the natural function for that which is unnatural, and
in the same way also the men abandoned the natural function
of the woman and burned in their desire toward one another,
men with men committing indecent acts and receiving in their
own persons the due penalty of their error" (Romans 1:26, 27).*

Sunday in Amsterdam. The sun is like a ball of fire,
resplendent in the infinite blue of the sky. Bright
tulips nod in the garden and adorn the party. Throngs
of people converse and celebrate. In the center of all
the excitement, holding hands and exchanging ca-
resses, the happy couple tells journalists details of their
recent wedding. The newlyweds say they plan to adopt
a child. From time to time they give each other passionate glances and smiles. The cameras of the international press record it all and send the news around
the world by satellite.

Such an event would attract little journalistic interest if the focus of such attention had been an ordinary
couple. But they were two men who had just come out
of the church after receiving a "nuptial blessing."

The event happened in Holland in 2001. Similar
incidents would later occur in Belgium, Canada, and
the United States. At first, people in many countries
protested them in defense of family values and morality. To many people it seemed like the end of the
world. Today, a few years later, "gay" marriages and
legally recognized civil unions of homosexual couples

are common in Argentina, Denmark, Germany, France, and Portugal.[1] And, as often happens, the newest fad soon becomes the custom, and the custom becomes part of the culture.

A recent parade of homosexuals and lesbians in Brazil brought two and a half million individuals into the streets.[2] The city of São Paulo had never seen such a large mobilization of people. It seemed like a carnival, happy and colorful with floats, and banners displaying slogans. The same thing is happening every year in other great capitals of the world. Homosexuals who formerly hid their lifestyle don't hesitate to take to the streets to advocate their position. They have rights, they say, just as everyone else. What is interesting and significant about this is the dramatic way in which it fulfills Bible prophecy. The Lord Jesus had said that in the last days such behavior would be part of the popular culture.

If the matter involved only people who have nothing to do with Christianity, it would be easier to understand. After all, someone who doesn't believe in the Judeo-Christian God has no biblical conduct to adhere to.

But even in Christian circles voices such as that of Mario Ribas defend the idea that "a sensible analysis of the Bible shows that all people, regardless of race, gender, and sexual orientation, were received by Jesus, and therefore, I don't see why homosexuals and lesbians are wrong in their way of being."[3] Ribas, a theologian, graduated from Princeton University in New England and is the pastor of a large evangelical church.

What is happening in the Christian world? Why

has something that the Bible classifies as sin suddenly become normal? Why have some started referring to the acceptance of homosexuality as "an expression of the grace of Christ"? The words of Jesus recorded in the Bible announce that in the last days it would be like this: "It was the same as happened in the days of Lot.... It will be just the same on the day that the Son of Man is revealed" (Luke 17:28-30).

How were the "days of Lot"? We find the record in the book of Genesis. The inhabitants of Sodom tried to break down Lot's door to seize two men who were guests in his home and to have sex with them. That is why the word "sodomy" is sometimes used as a synonym for homosexuality. In the days of Lot homosexuality was acceptable, and God showed His disagreement with that kind of human behavior (Genesis 19:1-11).

Jesus foretold that the last days would be like the days of Lot.

The Bible teaches that God loves everyone. Homosexuals, like every other human being, are objects of His love and mercy. But Jesus came to our world not only to forgive sinners but also to transform them and make them new creatures. The apostle Paul explains it simply: He gave life to you when "you were dead in your trespasses and sins, in which you formerly walked according to the course of this world," "indulging the desires of the flesh and of the mind, and were by nature children of wrath" (Ephesians 2:1-3). He goes on to declare that they were "darkened in their understanding, excluded from the life of God because of the ignorance that is in them, because of the hardness of their heart; and they, having become callous, have given themselves over to sensuality for the practice of every kind of impurity with greediness. But you did not learn Christ in this way, . . . that, in reference to your former manner of life, you lay aside the old self, which is being corrupted in accordance with the lusts of deceit, . . . and put on the new self, which in the likeness of God has been created in righteousness and holiness of the truth" (Ephesians 4:18-24).

Here the apostle speaks of transformation. Every human being, no matter what their sin is, needs to undergo the miracle of conversion. Conversion involves repentance, forgiveness, and putting off the old way of living. In the light of what the apostle Paul says, it is impossible to accept the politically correct idea that because God is love He will accept any and all deviations of human conduct.

God described His character to Moses: "The Lord, the Lord God, compassionate and gracious, slow to anger, and abounding in lovingkindness and truth; who keeps lovingkindness for thousands, who forgives iniquity, transgression and sin; yet He will by no means leave the guilty unpunished" (Exodus 34:6, 7).

The word "guilty" in the original language refers not to people who sometimes do what is evil, but those who insist on living that way.

Evidently social pressure to accept something that the Bible condemns is another fulfillment of the signs of the end. The open proliferation of homosexuality and the argument that it is just "a different type of sexual orientation" is an evidence that we live in the last days.

Some years ago the Natural History Museum of

Oslo presented an exhibit on homosexuality in the animal world.[4] It argued that if homosexuality exists among the animals, and seems perfectly natural among them, then sexual deviation is also natural among human beings—and if it's natural, then it can't be sin.

The dictionary defines the word "natural" as something done according to the property of things. The key word here is "property." What are the natural properties of things? It is natural to eat through your mouth. If I want, I can try to eat through my ears. I am perfectly free to do so, but I cannot expect people to accept my idea as something natural, normal, and proper.

Our generation has lost touch with its own nature. It lives almost entirely for physical pleasure. In the United States alone the fabulous sum of $13 billion is spent on pornography every year.[5] You can hardly turn on your computer anymore without receiving an invitation to look at pornography. Most of the music and movies written, composed, and produced now have sex as the central theme. You seldom find an advertisement that does not use sex appeal to sell the product.

What is the problem with this? Humans are physical, mental, and spiritual beings. They cannot be split into separate segments. In order for what people do in life to make sense they need to do it with the complete unity of their being. To divide or fragment is fatal. If they try it, they will open deep wounds in their subconscious—wounds that their rationalism cannot cure. No matter how often we tell ourselves that it's OK, that it's good as long as it doesn't hurt anyone, and that one's private life is a matter of personal choice or preference, the reality is different. A person's nature as a human being, with physical, mental, and spiritual faculties, cannot cope with this. It may be that, swept along by uncontrolled instinct, it can tolerate a distortion and perversion of its physical dimension, and perhaps our mental aspect can be convinced by its own arguments that this is acceptable; but the spiritual nature rejects it.

"I am not spiritual," a man said to me one day when I visited him in prison.

He was there because he had tried to live a life without restrictions. Although unwilling to recognize it, he was still a spiritual being. If not, he would not have insisted so much on having me visit him.

Humanity's problem in our time is that we do not recognize our spiritual nature. Nevertheless, the fact that we attempt to ignore it does not change reality. Spirituality is not something we choose to be or not be. It is beyond our control, because it came from the hands of the Creator. Our life will be complete only as we live in harmony with Him and respect the integrity and unity of how He made us.

Here is an illustration: Take a bird and put it in a golden cage covered with diamonds. Put plenty of food and water in the cage, and if you like, give it air-conditioning adapted to its needs. Do you think it will someday be happy? Never! It has a bird's nature and was born to be free—to fly. It is true that it needs water and food, but what makes it happy is freedom.

People think that they are free because they can do whatever they want, but they are prisoners of pleasure. Mario Veloso, poet, author, and personal friend, states that formal freedom is not enough to be truly happy. A country or government can guarantee freedom of the body, but not of the soul.

Those who live under totalitarian regimes suffer no more than those who live in societies with full freedom. Why? Because human beings are prisoners of their complexes, tendencies, selfishness, ambitions, envies, vices, and everything that constitutes the dark side of human psychology.[6]

Such captives can never be truly happy. In their frustration many of them turn to a life of pleasure and give free rein to immorality. Those who attempt to leave out the spiritual dimension of life are welding shut the bars of their own prison. As incredible as it may seem, the factors that most imprison modern people are, according to Veloso, obscenity, pornography, violence, and homosexuality.

David Levy published a book titled *Love and Sex With Robots.* After investigating the possibility of relationships between humans and robots, the author concluded that people unable to establish satisfactory relationships with other humans should substitute relationships with machines. He was not joking.[7]

Levy's intention may be all right; but for sex to be fully satisfying and make a person happy, it has to be a physical, mental, and spiritual act. If sex is only physical, it is frustrating and leads to emptiness and dissatisfaction.

So what do people do to respond to the cry of a needy heart? They plunge into all kinds of perversions and depravity. As the Bible says: "God gave them over to degrading passions; for their women exchanged the natural function for that which is unnatural, and in the same way also the men abandoned the natural func-

81

tion of the woman and burned in their desire toward one another, men with men committing indecent acts and receiving in their own persons the due penalty of their error" (Romans 1:26, 27).

What is the "penalty of their error" that the apostle here speaks about? He refers to all the plagues and illnesses that strike the modern world. A study carried out by the U.S. Center for Disease Control and Prevention shows that 19 million people in the United States become infected every year with sexually transmitted diseases, and more than 65 million live permanently with such diseases in their bodies.[8] AIDS is decimating humanity. At present, 43 million people live with AIDS. Last year alone it infected an additional 4.8 million. Worse yet, 2,000 babies acquire the disease in their mothers' wombs.[9]

The Bible foretold that all of this would be an indication that we are living at the end of time. Jesus declared: "Now learn the parable from the fig tree: when its branch has already become tender, and puts forth its leaves, you know that summer is near; so you too, when you see all these things, recognize that He is near, right at the door" (Matthew 24:32, 33).

It was late afternoon of a sad day as her life seemed to have come to its end. Her dreams had killed her. Men had condemned her as a flagrant sinner. Mistakes had filled her life, and she had loved in the wrong way. Although she had longed to be loved in return, she had only been used, leaving her with open wounds that no one could heal.

What can a person do or say when she knows that she has made a mistake and deserves to be punished for it? She can repeat again and again what she was already doing, so that the pain she believes she deserves will be even worse. The woman had chosen this way—one that plunged her to the bottom of the pit and made her feel like trash. Although she knew that she ought to change her way of life, she didn't have the strength.

It was then that the men had caught her in the very act of sin and dragged her to the presence of Jesus. She knew she deserved to be stoned. The implacable law offered neither mercy nor forgiveness.

There she was. Her past was ugly. Her present, horrible. And her future nonexistent. Then there appeared the wonderful person of Jesus. Thank God He always shows up just when we need Him most. That's how God is: He always looks for you, calls, and waits for your response.

The teacher from Galilee silently began to write in the sand, and the accusers of the poor woman disappeared one by one. Then the voice of Jesus broke the sudden silence. "He who is without sin among you, let him be the first to throw a stone at her" (John 8:7).

No one dared, and soon the street was deserted.

"Woman, where are they? Did no one condemn you?" Jesus asked.

"No one, Lord," she replied, not daring even to look up.

"Neither do I condemn you," the Lord told her. "Go. From now on sin no more" (verses 10, 11).

Twenty centuries have come and gone since that day. The voice of the Master is still heard coming down to us. His promise is: "Give me your heart, and I will make it new."

What a wonderful invitation! Do you believe it? What will you do about it?

The answer is yours alone.

---

[1] "Special Report: Homosexual Civil Union"; www.traditionalvalues.org/pdf_files/CivilUnions.pdf.

[2] "Marcha do Orgulho Gay 2007"; www.esquerda.net/index.php?option=com_zoom&Itemid=112&catid=31.

[3] Márcia Freitas, "Aceitação de padres gays é inevitável, diz reverendo brasileiro"; www.bbc.co.uk/portuguese/reporterbbc/story/2004/10/041019_reverendogaymp.shtml.

[4] "Against Nature? An Exhibition on Animal Homosexuality"; www.nhm.uio.no/againstnature/index.html.

[5] Adam Tanner, "Porn Industry Threatened by Video-sharing Websites"; www.huffingtonpost.com/2008/01/11/porn-industry-threatened-_81177.html; Jon Swatz, "Purveyors of Porn Scramble to Keep Up With Internet"; www.usatoday.com/techinvestor/industry/2007-06-05-internet-porn_N.htlm.

[6] Mario Veloso, *Libre para amar* (Buenos Aires: Asociación Casa Editora Sudamericana, 1984), pp. 19-28.

[7] David Levy, *Love and Sex With Robots* (New York: Harper Collins, 2007).

[8] "Report From the Centers for Disease Control and Prevention," *USA Today,* Mar. 25, 2008.

[9] "El SIDA avanza y el virus HIV llega a casi 40 millones de infectados en el mundo"; www.radioagencianp.com.br/index.php?option.

Eight

Economic Recession

> *"Come now, you rich, weep and howl for your miseries
> which are coming upon you. . . . Behold, the pay of the
> laborers who mowed your fields, and which has been
> withheld by you, cries out against you"*
> *(James 5:1-4).*

The city of São Paulo was dazzling that night as I stared across it from the balcony of the Italia Building. Entering the restaurant, I looked around. The receptionist, a tall blond young man with artificial manners, asked, as if he knew me, "Mr. Bullón?"

I nodded with a smile, and he took me to a private table in the rear. The person I was looking for was there, waiting for me. As he arose we exchanged greetings, and after a brief trivial conversation he got to the point.

"You know I have money," he said, taking charge of the situation at once. "I can buy whatever I want, travel to any place in the world, and make things happen that most people just dream about; but when night comes, I can't sleep. I feel as if I were in debt to someone. Some nights I remain awake until dawn. Tell me what I'm missing, but please don't ask me to become a member of your church, and don't talk to me about Jesus."

His attitude surprised me. Although a giant in the world of business, he sat there almost begging for help, but he didn't want me to talk to him about Jesus.

"You know that I am a minister," I said.

"Yes, but can't ministers talk about anything else but religion?"

"Of course we can. I could discuss the stock market or the present exchange rate for dollars. I could talk to you about sports or about the culture of the different countries I have visited, but you have just asked me a specific question. You want to know what you are lacking, and I am sure it is not stocks and bonds, travel, or culture. What you need is a spiritual sense for your life, but you don't want me to talk to you about Jesus. What can I do? If I were to tell you that the solution to your problem is in India and that it would cost you $1 million, you wouldn't hesitate a minute. You would get your private jet ready and go there immediately to look for the solution. Am I mistaken?"

The man blinked several times, took a sip of water, and didn't know what to say. He was aware of the emptiness of his life. Something was seriously wrong. At the beginning of his career, when he was still young and filled with dreams and ambition, he believed that he needed money to be happy. He concentrated all his efforts on getting it, and had achieved his objective. By now he was a multimillionaire and, according to his original plan, should have been satisfied—but he wasn't. Instead, he felt constant anguish and couldn't identify the cause. Although looking for help, he didn't want to hear anything about God.

We talked a bit more, then said goodbye without coming to any conclusion. The classic portrait of a modern man, he had made money his god. But in spite of all his money he was empty and distraught.

"Money is a powerful horse," says the proverb.

And people have always given themselves body and soul to getting as much as possible of it. "Money is the lever that moves the world," repeated the gold seekers as they risked their lives in the Amazon jungles searching for the precious metal.

The mad race for money dominates today's culture. It destroys lives, corrupts consciences, and leads to the overthrowing of governments. Yet people think that if they only had more money they would be happy, and therefore spare no effort or time to get it.

The man who spoke with me that night had discovered that money failed to bring happiness. But many, in their desperate attempt to fill the void that money cannot, fall into greed: the idolatry of money.

Greedy people live just for the getting. They accumulate riches they can't use. Afraid to spend and terrified of being poor, they never have enough. They care about no one but themselves. The apostle Paul describes this kind of people as one of the signs of the last days: "In the last days" "men will be lovers of self, lovers of money" (2 Timothy 3:1, 2).

The desire to accumulate riches makes human beings lose their sense of values. Things come to be more important than people. Always wanting to be richer, the wealthy will lie, exploit, extort, corrupt, and be corrupted without caring about others. Such individuals exist in every field of human endeavor: in business, in the government, and even in churches.

It is the poor and weak who especially suffer the consequences of the greed of others. Every day they have fewer opportunities and more poverty and misery. One evidence that the return of Christ is near is the increasing wealth of a few and the extreme poverty of so many.

According to the report of the United Nations Hunger Project, every second someone dies on the planet because of hunger. Seventy percent of them are children under 5.[1]

November 13-17, 1996, the World Food Summit convened in Rome. One hundred eighty-five nations sent their representatives. They proposed to end hunger by 2015. Since then hunger has instead dramatically increased.[2]

Most of the deaths caused by hunger result from chronic malnutrition. Families simply don't get the food they need to survive. The United Nations Food and Agriculture Organization (FAO) estimates that at least 820 million people suffer from hunger and malnutrition.[3]

The Bible says that in the last days the outcry of the impoverished would lead to terrible conflicts between capital and labor. The apostle James says: "Come now, you rich, weep and howl for your miseries which are coming upon you. Your riches have rotted and your garments have become moth-eaten. Your gold and your silver have rusted; and their rust will be a witness against you. . . . It is in the last days that you have stored up your treasure! Behold, the pay of the laborers who mowed your fields, and which has been withheld by you, cries out against you" (James 5:1-4).

Exploitation will turn those without God into loaded weapons, and time will pull the trigger. Hunger is the incubator of war everywhere in the world. Constant poverty and prolonged oppression drive people into aggression and terrorism.

The struggle to survive particularly affects those living in rural areas and the edges of the great cities. Seven out of every 10 poor people, some of whom earn less than a dollar a day, dwell in such places and are especially vulnerable to being recruited for revolutionary guerrilla movements that claim to promote social justice but, unfortunately, too often end up destroying what remains of the already impoverished economy of the underclasses. Other victims of poverty slide into drug trafficking and organized crime.[4]

Careful studies of the most critical social conflicts of our time reveal that in the poorest and neediest countries revolutionary convulsions and delinquency reflect a lack of economic programs to meet the needs of growing populations. People who for decades have been without any way to improve their lives reach the place where they can't stand any more, and they end up challenging all established authority.

The majority of the modern world's social conflicts have their roots in the sense of frustration, injustice, and desperation that more and more people feel. Mix in the widespread inequality and discrimination prevalent in many cultures, and you have the class struggle foretold in the Bible as one of the signs of the return of Christ.

To make matters even worse, people today are more aware of inequality and injustice than ever before. Almost everyone has access to radio, television, and other forms of communication. The media stimulate consumerism among those who have the resources to buy, while at the same time flaunting an ostentatious lifestyle beyond the reach of the great majority. The globalization of information feeds the growing anger of the neediest social classes.

No longer does most of the world just passively accept the old argument that most are destined to be poor and that they have no choice in the matter. Today people want to change the order of things. Unfortunately, they don't realize that armed struggle is not the remedy for the problem.

The social struggle continues. It is the result of injustice, avarice, and collective selfishness. But it doesn't stop there. When the apostle James said that the wages of the workers would cry out for what they had not been paid, he was also referring to strikes and labor militancy.

As I write these lines, strikes have swept the nation of Spain. The country is nearly paralyzed because public transportation workers are demanding better wages. The strike has extended to other sectors, including funeral services and the employees of the Ministry of Justice.

Germany recently went through a chaos in which the German labor union Verdi announced that it would continue indefinitely its service strike in airports and railways.

In the United States, General Motors announced the closing of a number of its plants and a cutback of production at others because of a strike at one of its principal suppliers.

The same thing happened in Brazil. The Rio de Janeiro police stopped work to demand better working conditions, while in Argentina the truck drivers' union sought better pay. People took to the streets in Peru to protest economic conditions. In Bolivia strikers armed with sticks were stopping traffic in five states.

Strikes constantly fill world news. The Bible long ago foretold the struggle between capital and labor. It is one of the signs of the return of Jesus Christ.

However, the Bible does not say that rich people will howl only because of the strikes. Economic turmoil keeps sweeping around the world. The United States has been going through one of the most critical times in its financial history. The stock market has gone through repeated ups and downs. Unemployment has risen, and families are losing their homes to foreclosure. In an emergency attempt to reduce the crisis, the U.S. Federal Reserve Bank repeatedly lowered interest rates until inflation became a threat, because of rising oil prices.

Many people in the United States keep asking: What is happening? Few know the greater dangers that could be looming on the horizon. According to Isaac Joseph, director of the Conference on Economics at the University of Paris, the uncertain situation of the three strongest economies of the world is one of the most frightening aspects of the present outlook.[5] Japan and the United States have been struggling with sluggish economies, and the outlook for Europe is gloomy. Under such conditions one cannot automatically dismiss the possibility of a worldwide economic recession. It is a financial tsunami that threatens to destroy everything in its path.

According to the specialists, the present alternatives are either a violent crisis or one that is less intense but more prolonged. And if this is a reality for the three greatest economies of the world, imagine what would happen to the developing nations that directly or indirectly depend on the stronger financial powers.

As is so often the case, it is the poor who suffer the most. At least they know what it means to suffer. Remember that approximately 800 million people go to bed hungry every night. But think about the rich, who have never known want and who cling to money as a source of security. No wonder the prophecy says they will howl—their riches will be useless to them.

When the U.S. stock market crashed in 1929, a number of millionaires lost everything in a flash, and a few ended up taking their own lives. It took years for the country to overcome the trauma.[6]

Money is important, but when human beings find themselves far from God they live permanently dissatisfied. Then wealth becomes an obsession. They cling to it as if it were the only source of security. But it is nothing but unstable sand.

Jesus said: "Everyone who hears these words of Mine and acts on them, may be compared to a wise man who built his house on the rock. And the rain fell, and the floods came, and the winds blew and slammed against that house; and yet it did not fall, for it had been founded on the rock. Everyone who hears these words of Mine and does not act on them, will be like a foolish man who built his house on the sand. The rain fell, and the floods came, and the winds blew and slammed against that house; and it fell—and great was its fall" (Matthew 7:24-27).

Dangerous times are coming. Financial winds are starting to blow across the earth. The Bible said that it would be so. When these times arrive, where will you have built your house?

The answer is yours alone.

---

[1] "Hunger Costs Millions of Lives and Billions of Dollars—FAO Hunger Report"; www.fao.org/newsroom/en/news/2004/51809/index.html.

[2] "World Food Summit Plan of Action"; www.fao.org/wfs/index_en.htm.

[3] "La FAO reitera su petición de fondos para alimentar a 400 millones de personas en 2015"; www.consumer.es/web/es/solidaridad/2002/06/14/47824.php.

[4] Tony Addison and S. Mansoob Murshed, "From Conflict to Reconstruction: Reviving the Social Contract," *Journal of Peace Research*. 40, no. 2 (2003): 159-176; "The Causes of Conflict in Africa" (DFID, 2001); "Development Cooperation and Conflict" (World Bank, 2001); "Report of the United Nations Secretary General on the Work of the Organization" (United Nations, 2000).

[5] "Speculation and Collapse: Enough!" *L'Humanité,* Mar. 27, 2008.

[6] "Wall Street Crash of 1929"; en.wikipendia.org/wiki/Wall_Street_Crash.

Nine

The Preaching of the Gospel

*"This gospel of the kingdom shall be preached
in the whole world for a witness to all the nations,
and then the end will come" (Matthew 24:14).*

The voice of the flight attendant woke me up. Glancing at my watch, I saw that it was 6:05 a.m., London time. In a half hour more the plane would land at Sheremetyevo Airport in Moscow. I was arriving in Russia to direct an evangelistic campaign.

As I looked out the window, trying to catch a glimpse of the Russian capital, there came to my mind the difficulties that people had faced in the old Soviet Union when they had wanted to study the Bible and serve God. Whoever had dared to preach the good news of Jesus ran the risk of going to prison. But the fall of the iron curtain and the *perestroika* of Mikhail Gorbachev had opened the door for the message of the gospel.

In 1992 pastor and speaker Mark Finley with an evangelistic team from the television program *It Is Written* did something that would go down as a landmark in the history of preaching. He held an evangelistic series in the Kremlin, the place where the former government had passed laws attempting to make God disappear from the lives of the Russian people. During Pastor Finley's meetings almost 3,000 people accepted

Jesus and were baptized. Today Russia is a fertile soil for the gospel seed. It is part of the fulfillment of another of the signs of the coming of Jesus: the preaching of the gospel in all the world.

Enormous challenges still remain, however. A number of countries and areas have yet to hear the saving message of Jesus. From a human standpoint it seems that for now, at least, it is impossible for the gospel to go to such regions. But as we look at the recent past and remember such places as Russia and elsewhere that were once apparently impenetrable and yet today are open, we have the assurance that one day there will be no place in the world that the gospel does not reach. The church is moving forward with strength in fulfilling its mission.

During the eight days I spent in Siberia I saw spiritual hunger everywhere. People fervently wanted to hear God's message. Every night I witnessed dozens of them accept Christ as their personal Savior. I saw them restored by the transforming power of Jesus.

The purpose of the gospel is to raise fallen men and women and return to them the lost image of the Creator. Human beings of all times and in all places have always needed the gospel. But if there ever was a time in history that we should preach the good news of Jesus with force, it is today. Never before have people been so desperate and lost in the shadows of their own reasoning. And never before have human beings sought so urgently to make sense of life.

Jesus loves such people and seeks to save them. He longs to show them the road to peace and joy. That is why one of the signs that tell us that we are living in the

time of the end is the preaching of the gospel to everyone everywhere: "This gospel of the kingdom shall be
preached in the whole world for a witness to all the nations, and then the end will come" (Matthew 24:14).

Right now, while you read these words, millions
of fervent Christians are going out one by one,
preaching the good news of the gospel in both cities
and towns and in remote areas of the planet. The Word
is going out through radio, television, and Internet, as
well as being printed in countless books and maga-
zines. Millions of people invite friends and neighbors
to their homes to share with them the word of hope.
They direct evangelistic series of all sizes and give
Bible studies in people's homes. The sign that Jesus
mentioned as an evidence of His return is being fulfilled in an extraordinary way.

In recent years I have traveled to different countries of the world to preach in stadiums, in the open
air, and in churches, rented halls, cinemas, theaters, etc.
I have seen how this prophecy has become reality as
people have been baptized by the thousands. They join
the church of God and express their desire to prepare
for the return of Jesus.

It was not only Jesus who mentioned the preaching
of the gospel as a sign of the time of the end. We find the
same message in the prophetic book of Revelation, in
which John records what he saw in symbolic vision: "I
saw another angel flying in midheaven, having an eternal gospel to preach to those who live on the earth, and
to every nation and tribe and tongue and people; and he
said with a loud voice, 'Fear God, and give Him glory,
because the hour of His judgment has come; worship

Him who made the heaven and the earth and sea and springs of waters'" (Revelation 14:6, 7).

The passage makes it clear that the gospel that the world needs to hear during the time of the end is not a modified message or something altered or watered down. The gospel that Adam and Eve heard in Eden is the same as that announced at Sinai. The good news at Sinai was the same as in the time of Jesus. The Master of Galilee preached the same gospel as the apostle Paul. The gospel of the New Testament is identical to that of the Middle Ages and our postmodern era. The good news that Jesus died on the cross of Calvary to save humanity was, is, and always will be the same.

What is the gospel? It is the good news of salvation. The center of the gospel is Jesus Christ—what He did, does, and will do for the human race. It is news of forgiveness and restoration. Humanity needs to hear it. Therefore God sends an angel flying in midheaven to preach this message to a suffering world now with more emphasis than ever.

Who is this angel? Whom does he represent? An angel symbolizes a messenger or a group of messengers.[1] The prophecy of Revelation 14 means that before the return of Christ God would raise up a group of messengers to proclaim the eternal gospel to the whole world. Prophetically those messengers would begin their activity after the persecution of the obedient church, a period that would last for 1,260 years.[2]

The prophecy says that the group of messengers would preach "with a loud voice." It means that the message is to be clear and distinct, one that might startle or alarm or even be politically incorrect, going against the thinking of the majority.

The message begins like this: "Fear God, and give Him glory." Why? Because the message has to be proclaimed at a time that human beings prefer to worship the creature rather than the Creator. It is for this reason that the angel points out the mighty works of God in creation. He emphasizes the sovereignty of God as Creator—that He is infinitely greater than the things He created. He "made the heaven and the earth and sea and springs of waters" (verse 7). Therefore, the creatures must direct their attention not to created things but to God Himself.

The messengers symbolized by this angel call on human beings to worship the Creator God. And they justify the demand by declaring that "the hour of His judgment has come." The world urgently needs to abandon the ways of idolatry and worship the only true God, because the judgment hour has come.

What judgment is it speaking about here? When Christians think of divine judgment, they generally look to the future. They relate the judgment to the coming of Christ and the destruction of the world. But the angel says that the hour of God's judgment has already come. Therefore, it cannot be a future matter, but one of the past and present.

The prophet Daniel describes the judgment in the following way: "I kept looking until thrones were set up, and the Ancient of Days took His seat; His vesture was like white snow and the hair of His head like pure wool. . . . A river of fire was flowing and coming out from before Him; thousands upon thousands were attending Him, and myriads upon myriads were standing before Him; the court sat, and the books were opened" (Daniel 7:9, 10). So you see, the "books" were opened to begin the judgment. A careful study of Bible prophecy indicates that it would commence in 1844.[3] Otherwise, how could Jesus reward the just at His second coming if He had not already examined the case of every person?[4]

Speaking of the judgment terrifies people. Even the thought of it makes them uncomfortable, because people equate the judgment with destruction. And if it is destruction, how is it part of the eternal gospel? The gospel is good news, not unhappy news. Most of us need encouragement, not fear, don't you think?

How should we view the judgment? Consider this: suppose that someone was trying to steal possession of your house. Both of you go to court about the problem. When the matter comes for the judgment, who needs to be afraid? You, who are going to get your house back, or the individual who has taken it away unjustly? Therefore, the judgment is good news for the just. For the wicked it is news that brings fear and desperation.

According to the Bible, the judgment is part of the gospel of salvation for a simple reason: the Lord Jesus, speaking of the Holy Spirit, said: "And He, when He comes, will convict the world concerning sin, and righteousness, and judgment" (John 16:8). Here we find the components of the message of the whole gospel. First, I am a sinner, and I can do nothing in my own strength to free myself from the condemnation to which my sins have subjected me. Second, justice comes only from Jesus. Therefore, He died for me on the cross and offers me freely His grace. Third, if I fail to take advantage of the marvelous provision of God's mercy and grace, I will have to give an account for my decision in the judicial process when I face the judgment bar of God.

Bible prophecy affirms that in 1844 two important things took place in the universe. The first took place in heaven. There the judgment began. The second happened on earth. God raised up a group of messengers to preach the eternal gospel, announcing that the judgment had begun and calling on men and women everywhere to renew their worship of God as the Creator.

This group of messengers formed a remnant church, the descendant of the woman of the Revelation (Revelation 12:17). The prophecy announces that God has summoned a church to give the last message to human beings. Because the church's mission is urgent, Scripture symbolizes it by the angel flying through the heavens. And because its message is important, the angel speaks "with a loud voice."

In order for such a church to fulfill its mission, God has been opening doors in recent years to enable for it to preach the gospel to millions around the world. Shortwave transmitters in strategic locations send the gospel message to practically the whole earth in many languages and dialects 24 hours a day.

Through them and many other communication methods, the gospel is reaching people even in the remotest and most distant places. The other day I received a letter from a man who said, "Pastor, I will never have an opportunity to meet you in person in this life. I just want to thank you because one day, over the radio, I heard the good news of the gospel as I listened to the message you were presenting. At that time my home was destroyed, and I had just made two attempts at suicide. I had come to the point that life made no sense. I was suffering a strange anguish that had plunged me into desperation. I couldn't sleep. I would pass hours of the night awake. I had gone to many doctors and specialists in emotional problems, but no one had been able to help me.

"Early one morning I turned on the radio and heard you preach. I had never believed in the gospel, Jesus, or the Bible. A rational man, I was an agnostic and considered religion something for weak people. I had no need for such crutches. But suddenly I don't know what had happened in my life. I began to lose the taste for everything. Nothing made sense anymore, and I was sinking deeper and deeper in a sea of despair—until that early morning when I heard you speak on the radio. In its darkness and silence the Spirit of God spoke to my heart, showed me reality, and made me see my need for Jesus. I accepted Him, and today I rejoice in sharing the news that has filled my life with people who don't yet know Jesus. I am a happy man."

The preaching of the gospel is fulfilling its purpose: to rescue people from death. The sign of the return of Christ is being fulfilled, and the world is being prepared for the final harvest.

Very soon, according to God's timetable, the day will come in which the Father will say to the Son:

"Go and bring home My redeemed children, those who believe in Me and are willing to obey Me even at the risk of losing their lives. I don't want to see them suffering, and I don't want to live any longer without them. The table is ready, the banquet is prepared. Only the guests are lacking. Please, go and bring them."

When that day arrives, will you be ready to go with Jesus?

The answer is yours alone.

---

[1] C. Mervyn Maxwell, *Revelation: Sus revelaciones* (Buenos Aires: Asociación Casa Editora Sudamericana, 1991), p. 90.

[2] Alejandro Bullón, *Tercer milenio* (Buenos Aires: Asociación Casa Editora Sudamericana, 1998), pp. 65, 66.

[3] Roy Gane, *Who's Afraid of the Judgment?* (Boise, Idaho: Pacific Press Pub. Assn., 2006). Most Christians have overlooked the fact that this judgment exists, and many of those who do have misunderstood its purpose. Gane shows in this book, based on the prophetic book of Daniel, that the pre-Advent judgment benefits the children of God. Daniel 7:22 says: "And judgment was passed in favor of the saints."

[4] Richard M. Davidson, "The Good News of Yom Kippur," *Journal of the Adventist Theological Society 2,* no. 2 (1991): 4-27. Davidson points out three principal reasons the judgment is good news: (1) it restores the gospel to its rightful place, and brings the believer to a position of assurance and vindication; (2) it achieves the purification of the heavenly sanctuary, where Christ is officiating; and (3) it vindicates the character of God.

Ten

A Strange Persecution

"Then they will deliver you to tribulation,
and will kill you, and you will be hated by
all nations because of My name"
(Matthew 24:9).

Two hundred forty human torches cast a horrifying light across the palace gardens. From his balcony the emperor Diocletian gazed with satisfaction on the scene of death. The agonizing screams of the Christians tore the air as they burned to death. Their only crime: to believe in Jesus Christ and obey His Word.[1]

Earlier Diocletian had ordered every copy of Scripture burned and churches torn down. Those who refused to renounce their faith were to be killed and their houses burned. History records that the emperor ordered a monument built with the inscription: "In honor of the extermination of the Christian superstition." It was one of the cruelest persecutions of history.[2]

The events of the first centuries of the Christian Era were sad fragments of a story that one would think would stand no chance of being repeated. But persecution appeared again in the Middle Ages. This time the Christian church itself persecuted groups of believers who insisted on studying and obeying the Bible as their only rule of faith and doctrine. Labeled as heretics, they faced judgment and death for their obedience to the Word of God (Matthew 24:9).

That was hundreds of years ago. Today it seems highly unlikely that someone would be persecuted for his or her religious convictions. Nevertheless, Jesus categorically declared that shortly before His return to earth a group of Christians would once again endure persecution, because of their insistence on obeying the Bible and the Bible only.

In chapter 5, when we looked at natural catastrophes, we saw that Jesus announced that extraordinary signs would appear in the sun, the moon, and the stars. "But in those days, after that tribulation, the sun will be darkened and the moon will not give its light, and the stars will be falling from heaven, and the powers that are in the heavens will be shaken" (Mark 13:24, 25). The Master stated that such things would happen "after that tribulation." What tribulation was Jesus talking about? He Himself explained: "Then they will deliver you to tribulation, and will kill you, and you will be hated by all nations because of My name" (Matthew 24:9; see also Revelation 12).

Does it mean that before the coming of Christ the world will experience a renewal of persecution? What type of persecution will it be? And what will cause it? No one who loves the truth can remain indifferent to this matter. It is something that has to do with the eternal destiny of every human being.

Before we go on with this subject, we need to remember that throughout history God has always had an enemy who has specialized in deception. He attempted to gain control of the human race through his lies. The book of Revelation identifies him as the devil and Satan (Revelation 12:9). John depicts him under the symbol of a dragon (verses 3, 9). The dragon uses seduction to achieve his ends. Through his lies he manages to deceive many, including, if it were possible, "the chosen ones" (see Revelation 17:14). But although seduction and deceit give him good results, there remains a group of people who study the Bible and don't fall for his deceptions. What can the enemy do with them? Overcome with rage, he persecutes them. What he doesn't achieve one way, he will attempt to do by another.

The book of Revelation speaks of that persecution, and Jesus mentions it as one of the last signs of His return to earth. John says that he saw in vision: "So the dragon was enraged with the woman, and went off to make war with the rest of her children, who keep the commandments of God and hold to the testimony of Jesus" (Revelation 12:17). Who is this woman persecuted by the dragon? Whom does she represent? In the Bible a woman often serves as a symbol of a church (see Revelation 12:1; Ephesians 5:25-32; 2 Corinthians 11:2). A pure woman, clothed in white, depicts the church of God (Revelation 12:1, 5). An impure woman, clothed with scarlet, stands for that part of the church that has become God's enemy (Revelation 17).

The persecuted woman is the symbol of those in the church who remain loyal to God. John himself described her in this way: "A great sign appeared in heaven: a woman clothed with the sun, and the moon under her feet, and on her head a crown of twelve stars" (Revelation 12:1).

This woman (church) has endured persecution from the dragon (Satan) throughout history. He attacked her with bitter hatred because she refused to fall for his lies. She held fast to the Word of God. John himself, exiled to the island of Patmos, is one example. It was there that he wrote the book of Revelation: "I, John, your brother and fellow partaker in the tribulation and kingdom and perseverance which are in Jesus, was on the island called Patmos, because of the word of God and the testimony of Jesus" (Revelation 1:9).

Notice two reasons for John's exile: The Word of God and the testimony of Jesus Christ. In reality, we could summarize both causes as one: his love of Jesus. If you love the Lord, it is logical that you will be faithful to His Word. And if you respect His Word, there is no way that will you accept the deceptions and lies that the dragon may invent. This makes the enemy furious. It is why he persecutes those who insist on obeying the teachings of the Bible.

Such persecution is not against those who merely carry the name Christian. If I am a Christian but I am ignorant of truth and follow the false teachings of the enemy, he has no reason to trouble me. He leaves me alone. Persecution is only for those who reject deception and insist on obeying what the Bible teaches.

The majority at that time will choose the path of least resistance. Meanwhile, those who cling to the teachings of the Bible will begin to be seen as radicals, stubborn, and politically incorrect. Could there be in our time anyone more worthy of rejection than a politically incorrect person? And whom could you call more politically incorrect than those who refuse to lower their values, who will not negotiate principles, who do not believe what the majority believe and refuse to accept what they accept?

The stubbornness of these persecuted people has to

do mainly with a matter that the great majority consider a foolish detail. In Revelation 12:17 the dragon persecutes the woman and also the "remnant of her seed" (KJV)—that is, the last-day church—because they insist on obeying God according to His Word. Notice that the church at the time of the end has two characteristics: it keeps the commandments of God and has the testimony of Jesus (Revelation 12:17; 14:12). They are the same reasons that led to John's exile on the island of Patmos— loyalty and obedience to God and His Word.

Today many consider God's commandments to be of no use to Christians. Many assume that the law was nailed to the cross of Calvary and therefore the Christian should no longer be concerned about keeping it. Nevertheless, the remnant stands out from the crowd precisely because they insist on being faithful to Jesus and obeying the commandments. It may seem like a trivial detail, but obedience to the eternal principles of the Word of God is not negotiable.

In Revelation 13 the dragon appears once again. Here he hands over his power to a strange new beast. In prophecy a "beast" symbolizes a kingdom or power (see, for example, Daniel 7:16, 17). John says of this new beast: "It was also given to him to make war with the saints and to overcome them, and authority over every tribe and people and tongue and nation was given to him" (Revelation 13:7).

The new power begins to persecute God's people. Since people worship it, it is obviously a religious power. "And all who dwell on the earth will worship him, everyone whose name has not been written . . . in the book of life of the Lamb" (verse 8).

According to the book of Revelation, during the last days a special religious power will acquire great authority. It will be loved and respected by multitudes, followed and praised by kings and princes. But at the same time it will persecute those who do not accept its authority and submit themselves to it. Who will reject the authority of the beast? Those who insist on being faithful to Jesus and His Word.

But notice: The prophecy also states that in the last days of our world there will arise a political power that will support the false religious one. It is the second beast of Revelation 13, the one that received its authority from the dragon. The apostle John describes it: "Then I saw another beast coming up out of the earth. . . . And he causes all, the small and the great, and the rich and the poor, and the free men and the slaves, to be given a mark on their right hand or on their forehead, and he provides that no one will be able to buy or to sell, except the one who has the mark, either the name of the beast or the number of his name" (verses 11-17).

People will not even be able to buy or sell unless they have "the mark of the beast." To understand this, it is necessary to know first the identity of the "mark of God." If it is true that the dragon marks his followers, it is also true that God does the same with His faithful and obedient children, the ones that He calls "saints."

Earlier John had declared: "After this I saw four angels standing at the four corners of the earth, holding back the four winds of the earth, so that no wind should blow on the earth or on the sea or on any tree" (Revelation 7:1). This refers to the final destruction of the earth at the second coming of Christ. Four angels hold back the winds of destruction. Why? The next verse gives us the answer: "And I saw another angel ascending from the rising of the sun, having the seal of the living God; and he cried out with a loud voice to the four angels to whom it was granted to harm the earth and the sea, saying, 'Do not harm the earth or the sea or the trees until we have sealed the bond-servants of our God on their foreheads'" (verses 2, 3). Notice that the angel tells the first four to hold back the destruction until God's servants are sealed.

Today, as you read this, we are standing at one of the most important moments in the history of the world, a fact that, sadly, few realize. Those who receive the seal of God will escape the final destruction, whereas John says that "if anyone worships the beast and his image, and receives a mark on his forehead or on his hand, he also will drink of the wine of the wrath of God" (Revelation 14:9, 10).

The book of Revelation depicts two great commanders. Both have their followers. And both identify their people. The dragon places the mark of the beast on his people. Jesus marks His with the seal of God.

But what is the seal of God? If we discover that, we can know the nature of the mark of the beast. A seal is an identifying mark. It carries the name or position of responsibility of the person and the extent of his or her authority.

Behind the seal of God lies His authority—His law and the eternal principles of His divine government. Behind the mark of the beast you can also find a supposed authority—the decrees and deceitful principles of the enemy. Behind the seal of God is His desire to save.

And behind the mark of the beast lurks the intention to destroy. Behind the seal of God are the Father, the Son, and the Holy Spirit, while behind the mark of the beast are the dragon, the beast, and the false prophet (see Revelation 16). The seal of God is placed in the life of those who "have washed their robes and made them white in the blood of the Lamb" (Revelation 7:14). The mark of the beast gets placed in the life of those who worship the deceiving power that claims to have divine authority without any right to do so.

The Bible contains a number of verses that explain the nature of the seal of God. One of them declares: "Sanctify My sabbaths; and they shall be a sign between Me and you, that you may know that I am the Lord your God" (Ezekiel 20:20). According to this passage, the Sabbath is a sign of obedience for the Christian church. God did not give the Sabbath to Israel alone. He instituted it at Creation (Genesis 2:1-3), and God's people observed it even before the Lord presented the Ten Commandments at Mount Sinai (Exodus 16:23-30). Jesus kept it (Luke 4:16). The apostles honored it both before the cross and then after Jesus was resurrected and returned to heaven (Acts 18:1-5). The author of the Epistle to the Hebrews says: "For He has said somewhere concerning the seventh day: 'And God rested on the seventh day from all His works.' . . . So there remains a Sabbath rest for the people of God" (Hebrews 4:4-9).

The enemy knows the Bible. He recognizes what the Word of God says. But he is a liar from the beginning, the enemy of the truth. So what does he do? Camouflaging the truth, he mixes it with a lie and then presents it using his method, which is seduction. The result: multitudes follow him, obeying and believing what he teaches. But another group of people love Jesus and obey His commandments. They are not deceived.

The price of obedience to the Word of God and faithfulness to Jesus will be a very high one. The dragon will vent all his anger against them. Using religious and political coercion he will initiate the greatest religious persecution of all time. Because it has been prophesied, there is no way to avoid it. It will be yet another evidence of the nearness of Christ's return. The prophet Daniel said: "There will be a time of distress such as never occurred since there was a nation until that time" (Daniel 12:1).

According to Jesus Himself, this persecution will take place before the great natural phenomena that will be manifested in the sun, the moon, and the stars. Luke tells it this way: "There will be great earthquakes, and in various places plagues and famines; and there will be terrors and great signs from heaven. But before all these things, they will lay their hands on you and will persecute you, . . . bringing you before kings and governors for My name's sake. . . . But you will be betrayed even by parents and brothers and relatives and friends, and they will put some of you to death, and you will be hated by all because of My name" (Luke 21:11-17). Notice the extent and cruelty of such persecution. Brothers and sisters will betray one another, as will parents and children, and friends will turn against friends.

It is true that, originally, Jesus was speaking of the persecution of Christians who would suffer under the Romans during the first century of the Christian Era, but it is also true that the persecution will repeat itself in the last days of the world's history. Remember that the Master was responding to the question that the disciples had asked with regard to the destruction of the Temple and the end of the world.

This last persecution will be the worst and cruelest of all time. Innocent people will be humiliated and made victims because they refuse to obey the dominant religious power. Political authority will enforce the campaign. And behind both of them will be the dragon.

Let's again consider the seal of God. As we have seen, the Bible says that it is the Sabbath, the day commonly called Saturday, the seventh day of the week. This brings us to the vital question of the nature of the mark of the beast. To understand it, we return to Revelation 13. Remember that it speaks here both of a religious power and a political power that "deceives those who dwell on the earth because of the signs which it was given him to perform in the presence of the beast, telling those who dwell on the earth to make an image to the beast" (Revelation 13:14).

Please notice that another symbolic figure now appears on the stage: an image of the beast. An image is a representation or symbol that stands for something else. When you think of the colors of your country's flag, it reminds you of what country you belong to, because behind the flag there exists a country. In the same way, if the authority of God expresses itself in a seal and the seal of God is the Sabbath, then what is the mark, the seal, that expresses the authority of the enemy of God? It must be something that counterfeits God's Sabbath seal—another worship day.

First of all, we must keep in mind that the Bible does not contain a single text that says the seventh day is no longer the true day of rest. At some point in history something appeared that pretended to have divine authority and changed the observance of Sabbath to that of a different day—Sunday. Many people sincerely believe that they honor Sunday because Jesus rose on that day. It is true that the Resurrection did take place on Sunday, but the Bible never says that because of that reason the Sabbath is no longer sacred and that now Sunday is the current day of rest and worship.

Sunday had a completely pagan origin. During Roman times sun worshippers regarded it as a special day. That is precisely the reason some languages call it *Sun*day.[3]

The observance of Sunday by the Christian church began many years after Jesus had gone back to heaven and after the apostles had died. Several factors led to it. One involved the struggle by the Jews who were trying to become free of Roman occupation. As the Roman authorities rounded up the Jews, Christians, who also observed the Sabbath, got caught up in the persecution. To avoid confusion, some Christians began to shift their worship day to Sunday. But the Bible provides no authorization for such a change.[4]

Sunday came to be officially accepted as a day of rest for the Christian church when the emperor Constantine accepted Christianity in the year 321. The influence of the emperor was decisive in establishing Sunday as a legal day of worship.

Today the Catholic Church accepts without hesitation its role as author of the change from Sabbath to

Sunday. An official publication of the church states: "Sunday worship is not based on Scripture but on tradition, and is a Catholic institution."[5] *A Doctrinal Catechism* confirms: "We observe Sunday instead of Saturday because the Catholic Church transferred the solemnity of the Sabbath to Sunday."[6]

The Church of Rome accepts responsibility for the change of Sabbath to Sunday. But there's more to it than this. While history records that the Church of Rome apparently made the transfer, the reality is something else. The true author of the change is the enemy of God.

A day of worship does not necessarily mean that that particular day is better than any other. It is not simply a matter of days. What really is at stake is what those days represent. The seventh day belongs to Christ. It is a sign of His power and His authority. He Himself declared: "So the Son of Man is Lord even of the Sabbath" (Mark 2:28). Through the prophet Ezekiel He also said: "Sanctify My Sabbaths; . . . that you may know that I am the Lord your God" (Ezekiel 20:20).

To honor the first day of the week as a day of rest is a human invention. It is an attack on the authority of Jesus. But to keep the seventh day is a sign of loyalty to Christ. Observing the first day of the week ultimately means disloyalty. If we will respect the Sabbath, we must walk in the way that Jesus did. Whenever anyone substitutes Sunday for the day that God ordained, they turn aside from the teaching of the Bible. The prophet Hosea reminds us: "Whoever is wise, let him understand these things; whoever is discerning, let him know them. For the ways of the Lord are right, and the righteous will walk in them, but transgressors will stumble in them" (Hosea 14:9).

As you look at the world you may feel that persecution as a sign of the return of Christ will never be fulfilled. Who would dare to persecute someone today for their faith? We live in a time of much religious freedom. The human race has never had greater respect for human rights. In much of the world countless social movements defend the rights of minorities. How would it be possible for someone to be persecuted only because they keep the Sabbath? From a human viewpoint it may seem impossible. Nevertheless, the Bible says that such persecution will be almost the last sign that will happen just before the glorious return of Jesus. It will be something surprising and unexpected. But it will be real.

Are you fearful of the persecution that Scripture predicts? You don't need to be. The Lord Jesus will take care of His faithful children. Read the marvelous promise regarding His infinite care for you: "Though youths grow weary and tired, and vigorous young men stumble badly, yet those who wait for the Lord will gain new strength; they will mount up with wings like eagles, they will run and not get tired, they will walk and not become weary" (Isaiah 40:30, 31).

Do you know what God will do for you besides taking care of you and giving you strength? Read what He Himself says: "For then there will be a great tribulation, such as has not occurred since the beginning of the world until now, nor ever will. Unless those days had been cut short, no life would have been saved; but for the sake of the elect those days will be cut short" (Matthew 24:21, 22). God personally promises you that He will shorten the time of suffering in the last days for the sake of His people.

All the signs of the return of Christ that we have studied so far have been in the process of being fulfilled. So will this one also, even though to many it may seem at first glance incredible. When the persecution comes, where will you be? To which of the two groups will you belong? Will you be with the persecutors or the persecuted?

The answer is yours alone.

---

[1] Marta Sordi, *Los cristianos y el Imperio Romano* (Madrid: Ediciones Encuentro, 1988), pp. 119-129.

[2] Ramsay MacMullen, *Christianity and Paganism in the Fourth to Eighth Centuries* (New Haven: Yale University Press, 1997), pp. 1-31.

[3] The *Deus Sol Invictus,* or "unconquered sun god," was an official state deity of the late Roman Empire. Several emperors before Constantine had ordered the imperial coins struck with the motto SOLI INVICTO COMITI, thus claiming the deity as a companion of the emperor. Constantine was especially devoted to this deity, and his coinage continued to bear legends relating to Sol Invictus until A.D. 323. On March 7, 321, Constantine decreed *dies Solis*—"Sunday"—as a day of rest.

The *Codex Justinianus* (3. 12. 3) reads: "On the venerable day of the Sun let the magistrates and people residing in cities rest, and let all workshops be closed. In the country however persons engaged in agriculture may freely and lawfully continue their pursuits because it often happens that another day is not suitable for grain-sowing or vine planting; lest by neglecting the proper moment for such operations the bounty of heaven should be lost" (http//en.wikipedia.org/wiki/Sol_Invictus).

[4] For Roman Catholic and Protestant statements about the Sunday/Sabbath issue, see www.amightywind.com/wolves/sabbath changed.htm.

[5] *Catholic Record,* Sept. 17, 1892.

[6] *A Doctrinal Catechism* (1957), p. 50.

Eleven

When Will Jesus Return?

"But of that day and hour no one knows, not even the angels of heaven, nor the Son, but the Father alone. For the coming of the Son of Man will be just like the days of Noah. For as in those days before the flood they were eating and drinking, they were marrying and giving in marriage, until the day that Noah entered the ark, and they did not understand until the flood came and took them all away; so shall the coming of the Son of Man be" (Matthew 24:36-39).

I grew up in a family of nine siblings. Our dad, a miner, came home only every two weeks. Before leaving He always left a list of things he wanted us to do before he got back. Although we had daily duties, we often would leave everything until the last minute. When the day finally arrived for Dad's return, we would divide the tasks among us and in a few hours have everything ready. Dad always thought he had marvelously obedient children. But he was deceived.

One day an accident occurred in the mines, and the company sent all the miners home, so Dad arrived back before we expected him. To his surprise, he found out the sad reality. His children were not as wonderful as he had thought.

My father was only human. He didn't have the ability to read the hearts of his children, but with God things are different.

A lot of people wonder that Jesus didn't tell us the exact day and hour of His return. I believe the reason lies in the nature of the human heart. If we knew the exact time, we would ignore His counsels about how we should live. Then a few hours before His scheduled appearance we would hurriedly try to get ready. But it wouldn't do us any good. That's why Jesus included the element of surprise. He Himself said: "But of that day and hour no one knows, not even the angels of heaven, nor the Son, but the Father alone" (Matthew 24:36).

Speaking of His return, Jesus said it would happen as in the days of Noah: "For as in those days before the flood they were eating and drinking, marrying and giving in marriage, until the day that Noah entered the ark, and they did not understand until the flood came and took them all away; so will the coming of the Son of Man be" (verses 38, 39).

There is nothing wrong with getting married. The fact that people marry is not a sign of the Second Coming. The central idea here is that Jesus' return will be a surprise. When it happens, people will be living just as they always have—business as usual. Only a few people will be paying attention to the signs of the times. That's how it was in the days of Noah. People were so occupied with just living that they had no time for God. When Noah began to tell them that the world as they knew it would soon end with a flood, no one believed him. They thought he was crazy and made fun of him.

The message of Noah was unpopular. To have accepted it would have been to expose oneself to a lot of ridicule. In the same way, today the message of the Bible is strange to the postmodern mind. Some people say it doesn't make sense. But then it was not different in the days of the apostle Paul: "For the word of the cross is foolishness to those who are perishing, but to us who are being saved it is the power of God" (1 Corinthians 1:18).

Noah preached for 120 years. At the beginning many probably believed his message. Some may have even helped in the construction of the ark. Others may have given funds and material to aid in fulfilling the mission that Noah had received. But the flood did not come as soon as the people expected.

Years and still more years went by. No one believed in a coming flood anymore. At the end, the only ones who were ready and went into the ark were Noah, his wife, and their three sons and daughters-in-law. That's all. Where were all the people who believed at first? They had gotten discouraged. Time had blown out the flame in their hearts.

Then one ordinary day, a day like any other, when no one was expecting anything different, something extraordinary did happen.

Something unusual appeared in the sky. A small cloud grew rapidly larger and darker by the minute, until it spread across the heavens from one end to the other. Thunder rocked the sky. Lightning streaked across the darkened expanse of the heavens.

Then everyone remembered Noah, the "crazy" old man, the ark builder. And everyone ran to the ark. They all asked to get in, but God had closed the door of the ark, and no human being could open it. The Bible states: "They did not understand until the flood came and took them all away; so will the coming of the Son of Man be" (Matthew 24:39).

Did you notice the emphasis in the text on people's lack of preparation? Before the Flood people weren't ready, and when Jesus comes back many will be in the same condition.

The apostle Peter says that before the Second Coming, history will repeat itself. "In the last days mockers will come . . . saying, 'Where is the promise of His coming? For ever since the fathers fell asleep, all continues just as it was from the beginning of creation'" (2 Peter 3:3, 4). Many will ridicule the idea of Jesus' return. Insisting that nothing strange like that will ever occur, they believe that things will continue just as they always have. As a result they will regard those getting ready for the second advent of Christ as if they were beings from another world.

In the following verses Peter tries to explain the apparent delay: "But do not let this one fact escape your notice, beloved, that with the Lord one day is like a thousand years, and a thousand years like one day. The Lord is not slow about His promise, as some count slowness, but is patient toward you, not wishing for any to perish but for all to come to repentance" (verses 8, 9).

Two thoughts especially stand out in Peter's statement. The first is the brevity of human life. How long can a human being live in our day? In Japan, Kaku Yamanaka died recently at 113.[1] But what is that many years compared with God's eternity? Therefore, Jesus' coming is not delayed. Human beings live no more than a millisecond compared with God's eternity.

The second thought has to do with God's mercy. He loves people. If it could all depend on His love, everyone would be saved, but salvation requires a personal decision. No one can interfere. God created men and women as free moral agents. He encourages them to choose. Although He has given them His Word to make the alternatives clear, the choice is theirs alone.

Nevertheless, the fact that God loves humanity and is patient doesn't mean that He will not return or that the day of opportunity will go on forever. Peter continues: "But the day of the Lord will come like a thief, in which the heavens will pass away with a roar and the elements will be destroyed with intense heat, and the earth and its works will be burned up" (verse 10). Here it is again—the element of surprise. Thieves do not let us know ahead of time when they will break in. We may know that they are lurking outside, but we cannot be sure of exactly when they will attempt to break in. Peter compares the return of Jesus to the unexpectedness of a robbery. The element of comparison he has in mind here is that of surprise.

What Jesus wants is for His children to be always ready. That's why He said: "Be on guard, so that your hearts will not be weighted down with dissipation and drunkenness and the worries of life, and that day will not come on you suddenly like a trap; for it will come upon all those who dwell on the face of all the earth. But keep on the alert at all times, praying that you may have strength to escape all these things that are about to take place, and to stand before the Son of Man" (Luke 21:34-36).

Some time ago I spoke with a person who knew nothing about the Bible. As we rode together in an airplane the conversation turned to spiritual questions. We shared the concept each of us had about life. I told him that I believed in the return of Christ and the establishment of His eternal kingdom.

"I prefer to live in the present reality," he told me. "Heaven is too abstract, and it's in a distant future. I don't know if I'll even be alive when that day comes."

A typical person of our time, the man thought only of the here and now. As far as he was concerned, it was not worthwhile trying to think about heaven while interesting things were constantly happening here on earth.

"Life is short," he told me in conclusion, "and we can't waste it on utopian dreams. We need to be realistic."

We need to be realistic? Then allow me to borrow an illustration from another writer. Suppose we live 100 years and come to the end of our days. And we discover that the man who spoke with me that day was right. Heaven does not exist. The coming of Christ is a utopian dream. There is no eternal life. Nothing. Then what will I have lost if there is nothing? Nothing! I will have lost absolutely nothing. But let's suppose that at the end of our days we discover that the Bible was right. Heaven is real, eternal life is a reality, and Christ does come back to take with Him those who are ready. Well, then, my friend in the plane will have lost everything. It's that simple. But it is also real and true.

Very soon a day is approaching that human beings will awake, just as they always have, to go about their daily round of activities. In factories employees will be carrying out their assigned duties. The clubs and entertainment centers will be filled. People will be doing good or evil, chasing as they always have after their dreams. Nothing out of the ordinary. Nothing different. Just as it was in the days of Noah.

Suddenly, in the midst of the sky, will appear a small cloud. It will grow larger by the second. The earth will shake to the very foundations. John described the scene this way: "I looked when He broke the sixth seal, and there was a great earthquake; and the sun became black as sackcloth made of hair, and the whole moon became like blood; and the stars of the sky fell to the earth, as a fig tree casts its unripe figs when shaken by a great wind. And the sky was split apart like a scroll when it is rolled up; and every mountain and island were moved out of their places. And the kings of the earth and the great men and the commanders and the rich and the strong and every slave and free man hid themselves in the caves and among the rocks of the mountains; and they said to the mountains and to the rocks, 'Fall on us and hide us from the presence of Him who sits on the throne, and from the wrath of the Lamb; for the great day of their wrath has come, and who is able to stand?'" (Revelation 6:12-17).

While some people are running around terrified, those who believed in the Second Coming and prepared themselves for that day will raise their arms and exclaim: "Behold, this is our God for whom we have waited that He might save us. This is the Lord for whom we have waited; let us rejoice and be glad in His salvation" (Isaiah 25:9).

One cold morning in a concentration camp during 1942 a young man looked through the barbed-wire fence and saw a girl that he thought was as beautiful as the sunlight itself. The young woman spotted him, too, and her heart leaped up. Wanting to express her feelings, she threw a red apple over the fence. Somehow the apple brought him life, hope, and love. As the boy picked it up, a ray of sunshine illuminated his dark world. The angelic face and the timid smile of that young woman lingered in his mind.

The next day he was eager to see her again. When he approached the fence, to his delight there she was. Waiting for the arrival of the young man who had touched her heart, she stood there with another red apple in her hand.

It was extremely cold, and the freezing wind moaned sadly. Despite that, two hearts were warmed by love as the apple crossed the fence.

The incident repeated itself for several days. Two young people, on opposite sides of a fence, briefly looked for each other. Only for an instant each day. The encounter was little more than a flickering flame.

One day the young man announced with a sad expression, "Don't bring me the apple tomorrow. I won't be here anymore. They are sending me to another concentration camp."

That afternoon the boy left with a broken heart. From that day on, the beautiful image of the girl would fill his mind during moments of sorrow. Her eyes, the few words they had exchanged, the red apple. For him it was a spark of joy in the midst of unending sadness. His family perished in the war and his life was nearly destroyed, but even in the darkest hours the image of the girl with the timid smile brought him joy, courage, and hope.

Years passed. One day in the United States two adults meet by chance in a restaurant and began to talk about their lives. "Where were you during the war?" the woman asked.

"I was in a concentration camp in Germany," he answered.

"I remember throwing apples over the fence to a young man who was also in the concentration camp," she recalled.

With his heart in his throat, the man stammered: "And did that young man say to you one day: 'Tomorrow don't bring me the apple, because they are sending me to another concentration camp'?"

"Yes, but how could you have known that?"

Looking into her eyes, as if he was gazing at a star, he said, "I was that young man."

A moment of silence. So many memories, so much nostalgia, such joy at seeing her again. The words almost refused to come out, but he went on: "They separated me from you that day, but I never lost the hope of seeing you again. Will you marry me?"

As he held her close she whispered in his ear, "Yes, yes, a thousand times yes."[2]

The world is a ripe fruit, ready to be harvested. Christ is coming back to put an end to the long sad history of sin. He is coming to take you home, coming to tell you that He never lost the hope of seeing you safe with Him for all eternity. There is a place in heaven for you, and it will never be the same without your presence. You are the most precious thing that

Jesus has on earth. Just as you are, with your joys and sorrows, with your struggles and conflicts, with your good points and mistakes—you are important to Jesus. So important that He came to die for you on the cross of Calvary, and is returning to take you home again with Him. Are you ready?

The answer is yours alone.

---

[1] "Japan's Oldest Person Dies at 113"; www.newsmeat.com/news/meat.php?articleId=17590794&channelId=2951&buyerId=newsmeatcom&buid=3281.

[2] Although subsequent events have revealed that the story is fictional, it still illustrates the human longing for hope—hope that only Christ and His second coming can fulfill.

If you are interested in knowing more about this topic and other Bible-related issues:

- Visit www.itiswritten.com to view a weekly Bible study program online and use the free online Bible studies.

- Find answers to hundreds of Bible questions in 16 languages at www.Bibleinfo.com.

- Explore Bible lessons, games, and stories just for kids at www.reviewandherald.org.

- Find more books on Bible-related topics at www.reviewandherald.org.

- Request Bible study guides by mail. Send your name and address to:
    DISCOVER
    It Is Written
    Box 0
    Thousand Oaks, CA 91359

Go DIRECT
to *Hope*

You'll find Christ-centered, family-friendly programs on
the Bible, spirituality, health, travel, history, finance,
education, and music on HopeChannel
—*now on DIRECTV channel 368!*

Switch from cable!
To subscribe:
888-393-HOPE (4673)

To support global Adventist television through Hope Channel, please call 888-4-HOPE-TV,
visit www.HopeTV.org, or send a gift to Hope Channel, PO Box 5303, Thousand Oaks, CA 91359.